How to Marry Money

How to Marry Money

The Rich Have to Marry Someone—Why Not You

Susan Wright

A Citadel Press Book
Published by Carol Publishing Group

A Citadel Press Book
Published by Carol Publishing Group
Citadel Press is a registered trademark of Carol Communications, Inc.
Editorial Offices: 600 Madison Avenue, New York, N.Y. 10022
Sales and Distribution Offices: 120 Enterprise Avenue, Secaucus, N.J. 07094
In Canada: Canadian Manda Group, One Atlantic Avenue, Suite 105, Toronto, Ontario M6K 3E7
Queries regarding rights and permissions should be addressed to Carol Publishing Group, 600 Madison Avenue, New York, N.Y. 10022

Carol Publishing Group books are available at special discounts for bulk purchases, sales promotion, fund-raising, or educational purposes. Special editions can be created to specifications. For details contact: Special Sales Department, Carol Publishing Group, 120 Enterprise Avenue, Secaucus, N.J. 07094

Manufactured in the United States of America

10 9 8 7 6 5 4 3 2 1

Library of Congress Cataloging-in-Publication Data

How to marry money : the rich have to marry someone—why not you? / Susan Wright.
    p. cm. — (the learning series)
    "A Citadel Press book."
    ISBN 0–8065–1693–3
    1. Mate selection. 2. Wealth. 3. Millionaires. I. Title. II. Series.
HO801.W87   1995
646.7′7—dc20   94–17840
                                    CIP

Contents

How to Marry Money

| *Introduction*

So you'd prefer to live a rich lifestyle...

Maybe you don't know how to go about finding a wealthy mate. Or maybe your self-doubts are keeping you from getting the sort of relationship you desire. Or maybe you can't get a commitment from a potential mate.

Well, with this book, you *can* marry rich.

You'll find out how to put yourself into a wealthy lifestyle where you can enjoy the people and things you deserve. You'll learn different ways to find a mate who gives you exactly what you want, including the commitment you choose. You'll also get tips on how to pursue someone, as well as ways to develop a relationship with someone who is wealthy.

You'll also learn:

- How to create a successful image
- Ways to meet people with confidence
- Where to go to meet wealthy people
- How to accept gifts
- Relationship pitfalls to avoid
- Ways to develop your sexual intimacy

For Both Men and Women

If you believe that love and marriage are all you need for a good relationship—then you need to read this book. Since marriage today is considered an equal partnership, the following advice can be used by both men and women. It can also be used as a guide for same-sex relationships.

Even if you don't want a mate who is fabulously wealthy, you'll find out how to get the relationship you want.

Unfortunately, most relationships tend to follow the same pattern. In the beginning love and passion carry us along, but they eventually degenerate into a struggle for power. As one partner becomes more dependent on the other, their possessiveness serves as a hold on their mate.

Developing a healthy relationship requires a fine balance between love (giving) and aggression (taking).

Be Practical

Less than a century ago women's economic dependence on men was a fundamental, unquestionable fact. Women were taught how to marry based on their mate's potential earning power.

Nowadays, though men have begun to do the same with women—taking into account their earning potential— women still have the edge in thinking practically about their mates. But this is countered by romantic illusions fostered by decades of movies and media misrepresentation.

Everyone should think practically when they are entering a partnership. Instead of focusing on desire and intangible signs of love, you can learn to make your choices based on what your potential mate truly has to offer.

Who Are the Rich?

Among the wealthy people of the world, you'll find the most successful commercial and industrial leaders of our time. Throughout history, they have directly influenced the development of customs and values in our society. They are also on the cutting edge of culture as patrons of the arts and contributors to political campaigns.

Wealthy people also know the value of other people. Maintaining and managing a fortune is complex, and millionaires depend on the skills and knowledge of people around them—from legal and financial advice to professional opinions on interior decorating and gardening.

Being rich can also be an attitude—a desire to enjoy the best things in life and explore what the world has to offer. Rich people are usually alert to their personal advantage in any situation.

If you are, too, then you can be rich.

What Is Rich?

There are many different ways of being rich.

Basically, if someone has a million dollars' net worth apart from a home, they are considered to be "rich." But rich doesn't necessarily mean a seven-figure net worth.

When you're assessing your needs, you don't have to put a number figure to your goal—it's a question of lifestyle, not accounting.

How rich is rich, to you? Do you want a big house along with the local country club membership? That's not *really* rich, but you could feel very rich indeed if that's the lifestyle you want.

There are also many people who are rich with potential— a wealthy lifestyle may or may not be in their future. You are rich with potential (and by using the techniques in this book, you can be rich), but you take a risk when you bet on someone else's earning potential.

Then there are those people who have been rich in the past. It doesn't matter whether they lost an inheritance or a business—these once-rich people usually have connections and, more important, the desire to be rich. With your help, it could happen again.

Why Do You Want to Be Rich?

In this book, you'll learn how to assess your needs and create goals that are attainable. You'll find that by focusing on your own desires, you can get anything you want. You can start to live rich right now.

So why do you want to be rich?

Time

Do you want the time that wealth brings? With the freedom of not having to work to survive, you can pursue a higher education, establish a career, or develop your creative talent. Or you might be interested in nurturing others with your riches.

Knowledge

The rich see more of the world than most people ever dream of. You may want to be rich for the travel and new experiences you can have, and the unique people you can come in contact with.

Luxury Lifestyle

Maybe you yearn for the rare and precious things that money can buy. Whether it's fine art or jewelry, culinary delights or pleasant surroundings, you probably have an image of the lifestyle you desire. Maybe you even want to give yourself the freedom to be lavish with those you love.

Business Sense

You could also associate with the rich to gain financial and business know-how. You can't expect to "feed" off someone—most people are adept at detecting parasites. Yet if you have a solid business venture in mind, and just need a boost to get on your way, you may be able to interest an "angel" in supporting you.

Prestige

If you want money for the social prestige or a lifestyle your old friends will envy, then you're simply indulging in dreams to satisfy your ego.

You won't find it easy to get anything when you're mostly concentrating on other people's reactions to your success. Certainly, show-'em-up daydreams can be a powerful goad, but that won't sustain you through all the hard work it takes to achieve any goal. And even if you do succeed, it likely won't be very satisfying.

How to Marry Rich

In this book, you'll learn how to achieve your goal of marrying rich, while fulfilling your own potential. You'll find out how easy it is to meet and marry someone who can give you what you want—all by building a firm foundation to live on.

This book will also take you through the steps of determining exactly what you do want. Then you'll learn how to live your life that way from this moment forward.

1 | *Focus on Your Own Life*

It's up to *you* to get what you want. To do that, you have to stay focused on your purpose in life.

What is your purpose in life? Do you want peace and stability in order to raise a family? Maybe you want to explore your creative potential, or you have a craving to delve into the high-stakes world of finance. Maybe you want to improve yourself, always learning and becoming the best you can be. Or maybe you simply want to be happy.

Your purpose in life can change with time, but let that purpose guide the choices you make as you are working to attain your goals—such as marrying rich.

Rich people are successful, and they appreciate success in others. Let your confidence come from your determination to fulfill your potential, and knowing that to succeed in attaining your goals, you simply need not give up. As long as you are true to your purpose in life, then you are succeeding. You are living a rich life.

Your Goal to Marry Rich

As with any goal, you have to make your goal to marry rich something you're working to achieve *right now*. To do that, let your purpose in life drive you forward, into the future, guiding your decisions.

Don't confuse your goal to marry rich with your purpose

in life. Sherry was one woman who made this classic mistake. Due to a lot of complicated reasons in her past, she decided that she wanted the security of a wealthy marriage so she could raise a family. Yet when we met, she was the mistress of a married man, and had been for many years. She had many of the trappings of the rich lifestyle, and was financially supported by him. Sherry finally left him because she realized he would never leave his wife and marry her.

Sherry had gotten so caught up in her goal of a wealthy marriage, that she forgot the reasons why she wanted it in the first place. If she had concentrated on her purpose in life—to raise children in a secure environment—she would have never spent the time on a man who was *unable* to give her what she wanted.

Your goal is not to find the "right" person, but to create the relationship you want. When you keep that goal in perspective—as a project that is fulfilling your purpose in life—you're less likely to get emotionally involved with people who can't give you what you need.

After all, there's a lot of people out there who don't want the same things as you. And like Sherry, you can't waste time fantasizing that maybe they will.

Maintain Other Goals

People sometimes make another big mistake by focusing on only *one* goal in order to achieve their purpose in life.

Whether it's your career, or your education, or your creative development—actively work toward goals other than marrying rich. If you have none, then get out there and start doing things to develop your own potential.

Even if you dedicate most of your time to pursuing your goal of marrying rich, maintaining other goals will keep you from placing too much importance on marriage.

Obsession

If you believe nothing else but marriage could satisfy your driving purpose in life, then you'll end up being half a person waiting for someone to come along and fulfill you. Too much will depend on every encounter you have, as you obsessively wonder—is this the one, is this my future mate?

Even if you try to appear casual, you'll never be able to hide your overwhelming interest, and that's self-defeating.

Yes, you must be open to the time and effort it takes to develop a committed relationship, but it can't be the basis of your happiness. You're falling into this trap whenever you're counting on your life being better once you've found your mate.

You have to actively work to make your life what you want it to be *right now*.

Examine Your Needs

Your needs are very specific, and you need to examine your own desires in depth. Think about not only the things that will satisfy you, but the things that you intend to avoid.

The best way to get what you want is by being practical about potential mates. Sure, we'd all like to fall gloriously in love with sparks flying whenever we touch.

But the kind of love you want is only real when it lasts, and that takes time. When you let your passion dictate your actions, you can end up broke and beaten.

Accept Your Desires

It doesn't matter if you want a relationship that is completely unconventional or if you're looking for the sugar-daddy of your dreams, the best thing you can do for yourself is accept who you are and what you want. Only then can you go out and get it.

Making Choices

When you're making choices, always remind yourself of your purpose in life. But don't make the mistake of limiting your choices because of your goal to marry rich.

Be open to everyone for their potential in helping you fulfill your purpose in life.

There was one man who almost refused to go out with one woman because she wasn't wealthy. But at his friend's urging, Mark got to know the woman. Then she introduced him to an agent who got him a part in an off-Broadway show. That show led to more jobs, as well as introductions to more people.

Mark says now that the friend who introduced him to his current (wealthy) wife can be traced to that first woman he didn't want to meet. He almost bit off his own nose to spite his face by limiting his choices.

Your Past

You must realistically look at your past experiences in order to understand what you truly want in your future.

School and Jobs

Take an honest inventory of yourself and your past goals.

Ask yourself—Do you have a history of switching jobs? Did it take you more than four years to finish college, or did it take you three?

This will tell you how good you are at pursuing your goals. If you have a history of getting sidetracked, then it's especially important for you to keep your overall purpose in mind. Don't allow yourself to pursue relationships that don't offer what you need.

Relationships

If you're like most people, at one time in your life, you've actively pursued a relationship that failed.

Ask yourself—Does it continue to haunt you? Or do you feel you learned from that experience? Which relationships were successful in terms of benefiting you emotionally and materially? What were you looking for then compared to what you are looking for now?

Also, are there patterns in your past relationships? After years in therapy, one woman realized she'd been playing out her relationship with her father over and over again. Yvonne would pursue unattainable men with a devastating combination of playing hard-to-get, while focusing her entire life around their needs. This left her anxious and unhappy, while the relationships were emotionally empty.

If there's a pattern, even a faint one, you might do yourself a favor and talk to a professional therapist. If you know the habits that have kept you from good relationships in the past, you can learn to prevent it in the future.

Conflicting Desires

We all have our daydreams, some of which seem to conflict. You may want romance and excitement, and at the same time want stability and security in your life. Which is more important, and when are both desires compromised?

Say, for example, you've decided your three main goals are to marry rich, have children, and be the best painter you can. One good way to judge the order of importance is relative to your age. If you're twenty-three, travel—to get exposure to the great artists in history—can come first in your goal schedule. Yet if you're already thirty-five, those children (especially for women) start to take precedence over everything else.

You also have to be realistic. Sometimes the things you value are difficult to find.

For example, if you insist that your mate have liberal, socialist views, then it's more than likely he or she won't be rich. Or if you don't want to leave your hometown, you may have a smaller pool of potential mates. And if you want someone who's in the same age bracket, it may be difficult for you to marry rich.

Wealthy Men

It's difficult to generalize about people, and wealthy people are even harder to pin down because of the vast amount of options money brings. But there are a few things to keep in mind:

Young men who have inherited money are usually out there enjoying it—there's no need for them to hurry up and settle down. So if marriage is your goal, you're fighting an uphill battle. But if you simply want to enjoy a wealthy lifestyle, then go for it.

Self-made millionaires are often too busy making money while they're young. It's only in their thirties that most start thinking about a family, which then prompts their marriage search. And then, they usually choose a mate who is younger.

Men who are divorced or widowed are usually in their late thirties, forties, and older. According to Masters and Johnson, men remarry much more quickly than women after being divorced or widowed.

A once-married, wealthy man is the most willing potential mate you can find.

Wealthy Women

Wealthy women have usually either inherited their money from their family or a previous husband.

Women can also become rich from a divorce settlement. Typically, once-married women are at least in their late thirties, more likely their late forties or fifties. These are the type of wealthy women you'll encounter the most.

If you have a yen for rich heiresses, it might be more difficult to marry rich. Women who inherit wealth are usually concerned with their standing among a select social community. Breaking into that often takes more than money —you must have some sort of celebrity status or family connections you can lean on.

Of course, there's that prized minority of wealthy women who have made their fortunes for themselves. These women are quite successful in getting anything they want, so if they want *you*, consider yourself fortunate.

Impossible Standards

Sometimes people sabotage themselves, setting up impossible standards in order to avoid intimacy. Are you using the image of a fairy-tale life to keep you from making a commitment elsewhere?

If you keep ending up in unsatisfying relationships, or if you keep pursuing people who are uninterested or unable to get married, you're letting the image of what you want overshadow reality.

Nobody will be able to meet all your desires. If a potential mate gives you kindness, respect, and fulfills your monetary needs, that's all you need. Once you start expecting your lover to possess every characteristic of your "perfect mate," you risk destroying perfectly good relationships.

2 | *Your Image*

The rich are often called the "beautiful people." But that doesn't mean they have striking faces and perfect bodies.

People are beautiful when they are comfortable in many different situations and when they enjoy interacting with other people. They are also beautiful when they treat themselves to the best things in life.

You can be beautiful by making the most of what you have. Know your own body, keep healthy, and feel good about yourself. That's the magic combination that makes someone compellingly attractive.

Your Attitude

More than anything else, the way you present yourself will determine how you are treated by others. If you are confident and open to others, people will respond with interest and respect.

If you're ever tempted to despair or quit trying because achieving a goal is too difficult, remember that as long as you're trying, success is in sight. When you quit, you're not pursuing the opportunities that could give you what you want.

Confidence

If you avoid eye contact and duck your head as you walk

through a room, you're telling everyone that you aren't worth their notice.

Practice feeling confident and positive, even if you have to fake it. Consider it an attitude adjustment. If you smile, it triggers an emotional reflex that makes you feel better. In the same way, if you hold your shoulders straight and look people in the eye, then you will start to feel more confident.

Focus Outward

One of the easiest ways to interact confidently with people is by focusing your attention outward.

Be aware of the people around you. Notice the way they carry themselves, how they talk, and the details of their clothing.

Pay attention to body language, as well. Someone who sits facing the room with their arms uncrossed is signaling their availability. Women tend to cross their legs higher when they're interested in someone.

Most of all, take note of how people interact, particularly the ones who who draw the most attention. They are the successful ones. They are the ones you want to meet.

If you see someone who looks interesting, make sure they see you too. But after a glance or two, deliberately avoid looking in their direction. Give them time to get interested in you. If you're *always* watching them, they won't be able to watch you.

Your Body

The most important aspect of your physical appearance is your belief in your own beauty. You have to love your body to be truly beautiful.

Other than that, laughing is the most alluring thing you can do. When you're happy, it lifts your energy and makes you beautiful.

Insecurity

No matter what you look like, people who are overconcerned or insecure about their physical appearance are unattractive. But if you love yourself, other people will too.

Even the most attractive people have to contend with their insecurities and self-conscious ways. We all reveal ourselves with nervous gestures like fussing with our hair, or looking in mirrors.

One woman told me she was a late bloomer—Patricia didn't develop her own style of beauty until her late twenties. Now she wishes she'd believed in herself sooner, because that was all it took. Once she accepted herself, she was able to make the most of what she had.

Affirmation

It doesn't matter if, according to society's standards, you're fifteen or fifty pounds overweight. It doesn't matter if you're eighteen or sixty. You can make yourself appear attractive as long as you stop asking for affirmation.

Also, nobody likes to listen to people moan about their diets or complain they can't do anything with their hair.

Even as someone tells you that you look great, or that your clothes are fine, their estimation of you has gone down. So don't even hint for compliments.

Once you relax and accept the fact that there'll always be someone better looking around the corner, then you can stop looking for affirmation. Then you can enjoy being the best that you can be.

Be Positive About Yourself

It's true that others will inevitably accept your own attitudes about yourself.

If you believe you have a great, sexy body that's just dying for your lover's touch, you'll be extremely touchable. But if you're self-conscious and try to camouflage your "flaws" then it's likely that negative attention will be drawn to those very things.

By accepting even the things about your body that you dislike—heavy thighs or thinning hair—you'll be able to start working with what you've got instead of against it. After all, how can you improve on something if you've rejected it outright?

Even the attributes that seem like a permanent cross can become features you prize. You can learn to rethink your opinion of your nose, or your height, or even the way your ears stick out. There are many people out there who may think that very trait is perfect—but they'll love you for it only if you do.

One man transformed his social life by following this piece of advice. Barry fought his receding hairline through his twenties and into his thirties, thinking that it made him look old. Finally he faced the inevitable and stopped getting unattractive haircuts that brought hair forward in bangs to disguise this "defect." He trimmed his hair neatly in the front, and let it grow slightly longer in the back to maintain a youthful air.

By working with what he had, he was able to find a hairstyle that gave him the effect he wanted. Women were much more attracted to him, which gave him even more confidence.

Be Natural

Your skin can be your biggest attraction. Protect yourself when you're in the sun.

And keep your face and hair scrupulously clean. That can do more toward creating beauty than trying to hide your flaws.

Besides, most of us don't have much patience for other people's pursuit of beauty. Vanity comes off as superficiality, and when someone pays too much attention to their appearance it betrays their insecurities.

Makeup

For some women, it's easy to fall into the habit of using makeup like a defensive mask, hiding the things they don't like about themselves.

But without realizing it, you can overdo makeup and perfume. People generally don't like to see a lot of makeup on women, particularly foundation, powder, and blusher. And while heavy lipstick or gloss may make you look more dramatic, you're much less kissable.

Pamper Yourself

If you believe you deserve the best, you'll get the best.

Treat yourself to facials and massages—you can afford to do it at least once a year. Getting a facial can be more than therapeutic for your skin. It can revitalize your whole outlook.

Get a Makeover

Both men and women owe it to themselves to learn how to enhance their natural attributes. Don't hesitate to experiment with your makeup or hair—change the style, even the color with temporary dyes.

It's also helpful to get professional makeovers every few years. You'll get tips about your sort of skin and facial shape. But don't put too much reliance on department store makeovers—salespeople are there to sell things.

It's only by trying different things, and taking risks, that you'll find the styles which suit you.

Get Color-draped

Everyone should get color-draped to determine the tones that best suit their skin and hair.

Colors do make a dramatic difference in the way you look. I've seen a pale green shirt bring out the glow in a woman's cheeks, making her look younger and more alive. But when a swath of hunter green cloth was draped over her shoulders, everything changed. Her features seemed to wash out, become dulled and flattened. It was the same lighting, the same woman, the same makeup—but the color of her clothes determined how she looked.

You'll be surprised when you see it on yourself—certain tones do bring out the best in us. Once you know ones that do, it's easy to incorporate that into your purchasing.

Clothing

You can always buy the latest magazines to find out the current style to wear and how to wear it. Namely, for men, *Esquire* and *GQ* and for women, fashion and beauty bibles such as *Elle*, *Allure*, and *Vogue*.

But none of that will do you any good until you know what looks good on *your* body. Just because something is expensive or trendy doesn't mean it's right for you.

Try Things On

Shop to find what what looks good on you. Go to the best boutiques and get used to trying on a lot of things—without even considering buying anything.

Try on clothes that are completely out of your price range. Not only will you find out the difference between quality clothing and mass-market apparel, but you'll be able to see exactly what flatters you and what doesn't.

You'll soon find the styles that suit you best. Besides, it's easy to look good in quality clothing. You'll feel better about yourself, when you're actually dressed the way you've always imagined.

The same goes for jewelry stores. Go in and try things on.

What would you buy first if you could afford it? By doing this, you'll train your eye to be discriminating.

Purchasing

Save up to buy quality clothing. The basics—a black dress or a good suit—are essential. But also buy things with a little flare. If you can't have variety, you can have clothes that make a statement.

Focus on body-conscious clothing that sends a subtle signal of availability. This doesn't mean tight or revealing—but clothes that compliment the natural shape of your body.

When you do buy cheaper clothing, chose the nicest materials. A simple silk shell may only cost $20, but it's indistinguishable from one that costs $120. Other quality materials include suede, wool, linen, and raw silk.

Also, if you want real jewels, then don't settle for costume jewelry. Save the money you'd spend on necklaces and earrings, and buy a strand of pearls or diamond studs. You'll have far fewer accessories, but the ones you have will be genuine. And, as your collection slowly grows, you'll become accustomed to saving and then buying one splendid piece at a time.

Thrift Stores

Thrift stores can be gold mines—or they can be as horrible as a walk through the city dump at high noon.

You'll have to find the thrift stores in your area and dive in there to see for yourself. The wealthier neighborhoods will usually be solicited by charity and hospital thrift stores. These can have beautiful designer clothing at a fraction of the cost.

Even in the most dismal stores, the constant turnover of merchandise almost guarantees that some gems will float through. Will you be there to find them? Devote your shopping time to only the best ones.

One woman got to know the salespeople in the best thrift store. Melissa says it's best to be friendly, without imposing on their time. She let several of the staff know what sorts of things she was interested in—even pointing out items at the cash register as she paid. One of the saleswomen eventually held back a Chanel suit that she knew Melissa would love. Of course, Melissa snapped it up.

Salespeople can also be helpful in pointing merchandise out to you. They know the store better than anyone, so rather than waste time rummaging through everything yourself, utilize their knowledge.

Your Name

If you really want to change your image, you can always change your name.

People have various names throughout their lives—nicknames when we're young, and pet names with our lovers.

Even now, you can come up with a new twist to your name. If you've always been Kathy, then try introducing yourself as Kate. If your name is Simore, call yourself Si instead.

It may make you feel stronger, more confident. And it might remind you that you've left behind the old mistakes and are starting fresh.

3 | *Meeting People*

If you've decided you want to marry rich, you'll have to put yourself among those who live a rich lifestyle. Simply by coming in contact with them, they become your potential mates.

If you aren't good at meeting people, you may simply need to learn a few social skills. That doesn't mean you have to pretend or play games, but there are certain types of behavior that can help you meet people.

And don't be intimidated. More often than not, the only thing holding you back is you.

If doing certain things feels uncomfortable, then it's up to you to overcome the fears that are stopping you. You have to practice new behavior in order to change the way you feel.

Interaction skills are easy enough to learn, all it takes is persistence.

Go Places Alone

You may be self-conscious at first, being alone. But you can use that feeling as an impetus to chat with other people.

The more often you go out alone, the more confident you'll become. Start by going to coffee shops or shopping alone. You'll soon find out that it doesn't matter if you're in a room full of strangers or a room full of friends—everyone becomes a potential ally.

All it takes is a little effort on your part, a smile or casual nod to make the first contact.

Nondiscriminatory Friendliness

Be equally friendly to everyone. It doesn't matter if it's the man who shines your shoes or the president of your bank.

"Saving" your charm for only potential mates is the quickest way to isolate yourself from everyone. The people you target will quickly be able to sense that your interest is peaked when you employ your charm on their behalf. Then, even sincere interest can seem phoney. Nobody wants to feel as if you're trying to fit them into your little mold of the "ideal mate."

Instead, open yourself to meeting both men and women. That keeps your interest level where it should be—warmly casual rather than "seeking."

And remember, people often meet their mates through friends. The more friends you make, the more opportunities you create for yourself.

Eye Contact

For most people, making eye contact doesn't come naturally. But you can learn how to be comfortable when you look someone right in the eye.

The easiest way to practice is when you're walking down the street. Walk as if you know exactly where you're going, with your head up and your shoulders back. Your expression should be pleasant, but don't paste a grin on your face. Your attitude should be relaxed.

Now, look at each person who walks by. Don't make it a quick, fearful glance. Hold their eyes for two seconds, getting a good impression of their face and attitude. Then casually slide your gaze back in the direction you're walking.

If you see someone who appeals to you—man or woman—smile as you start to look away. It can be very effective if they notice.

The more you practice making eye contact with strangers, the more comfortable you'll be going into any unknown situation.

Speak First

Simple greetings and casual friendliness will enable other people to approach you. It also spreads a general feeling of good fellowship wherever you are.

Remind yourself to meet people's eyes, keeping your expression relaxed, even smiling slightly as if you've just heard good news.

Then, as you walk past people, drop casual comments about the event, or say hello. You can say anything that is brief—whatever you can fit into a pause while you're moving from one place to the next.

People are always more willing to respond to a stranger who seems amiable and relaxed. But don't come on strong—a brightly false front will be avoided by most people as their defenses instinctively rise.

As long as you make it clear you aren't going to linger or impose, people will usually respond to your comments positively.

Make Conversation

It doesn't take much to create a conversation with someone. All you have to do is comment on anything that's happening or something you see.

For example, if you're at a party and you're approaching a woman who's looking at the flower arrangements, you could say in passing, "Aren't they gorgeous?" Her response will probably be positive since you've noticed something that's already interested her.

Ask Questions

Once you've made contact, keep asking questions. Especially ones that can't be answered with a simple yes or no. Then you've got a conversation on your hands.

For example, now that you've gotten the woman's attention by commenting on the flowers, you can follow up with another question that isn't so easy to answer, such as, "Which ones do you like?"

Maybe she'll tell you she likes the tiny white daisies, or the vibrant colors of the bird of paradise—whatever it is, you can learn a lot about someone by asking questions.

Focus on Them

Talk about them and what they think is important. It's extremely flattering. Even if someone leaves the conversation knowing nothing about you or your preferences, you'll be remembered as truly charming.

Do try to find some common ground as quickly as you can—this creates the foundation for further interaction.

End the Conversation First

Whatever you do, when you initiate the conversation, make sure you are the first to end it and move on. Don't wait until there are signs that someone is getting tired of talking to you.

That always leaves people wanting more. Then the next time you see them, they'll want to talk to you again.

Practice

Like anything else, it takes practice to present yourself the way you imagine you could be.

Focus on one thing at a time, and be patient. Transforming your behavior takes repetition and plenty of time, exactly the same way you have to work to break bad habits.

The only thing that matters is that you *can* change.

At first, you might hate making eye contact with pass-ersby, or chatting with the checkout girl. Ignore those feelings— you've let them stop for you too long.

Keeping an open, positive attitude will always create opportunities for you to meet people. You'll get used to talking to strangers.

Once you see how easy it is, you'll want more.

4 | *Live Rich*

If you truly desire the best, then make an effort to get it for yourself by immersing yourself in the wealthy lifestyle. When you do, you'll be in the company of others who also enjoy the finer things in life—and those are the people you want to meet.

After all, the key to getting anything is by living your life as if you already have it. You have to stop waiting for someone else to come along and do the "right" things. You have to want it so badly that you're willing to give up whatever stands in your way.

Just because you might not be adept at first—dealing with etiquette, or handling things that are expensive—that doesn't mean you can't learn. It's a matter of accustoming yourself to luxury, and training yourself to be discriminating.

Live Among the Rich

If you want to meet people who live a certain lifestyle, then the best place to live is in their neighborhoods.

Even if you have to rent an apartment in the basement or put up with less space than you could get elsewhere—live where the rich live.

Then, your neighbors and the people you interact with on a daily basis—when you buy gas or go to the bank—will be the kind of people who live the lifestyle you desire.

You may think you have a better standard of living by staying in a nicer place in a low-rent area, but you're programming yourself to always stay at that level. If you keep your eyes on the best, you'll always get more than if you settle for what you've got.

Go to Chic Neighborhoods

If it's impossible to live in the most expensive neighborhoods, then live nearby so you can go there.

Become familiar with the area, shopping in the local supermarket and specialty stores. Walk or jog only in the best areas. And join the neighborhood gym—but only if you can work out during the day.

Any sort of daily contact you have with rich people will create opportunities for more interaction.

Working Among the Rich

If at all possible, work where you can meet the kind of people you'd like to socialize with.

If you're a nurse, apply for jobs at the most prestigious hospitals. If you're a lawyer or a dentist, set up practice in the wealthier neighborhoods. If you're in accounting or management, then jobs in financial institutions such as banks, real estate, and brokerage firms can bring you in contact with successful entrepreneurs.

The Service Industry

If you have no special training, then by all means get a job in the service industry in or near the most expensive neighborhoods. There's a multitude of service jobs available—from hotel staff and waitressing, to working as a clerk or a parking lot attendant. If you have to, work your way up to the nicer establishments.

Not that it's easy to make that leap from "servant" to

potential mate. People pay for unobtrusive service and they don't want to interact with you. In their minds, the pool man cleans the pool, and the nanny takes care of the kids— and that's as far as it goes. Unless you make the effort to change their attitude.

Your attitude and approach will make or break you.

There was one woman who was quite successful this way. Kay didn't consider herself to be very smart, but she was quite pretty when she was young and decided to make the most of her looks rather than pursue a college degree. She took a job as a cocktail waitress during "happy hour" at one of the best bars near the financial district. There she met stockbrokers and bankers by the dozen, and by focusing on the men who had similiar goals as she did—marriage and travel, she eventually launched her first rich marriage.

A Rich Boss

It's never a good idea to date the people you work for, but your position does give you opportunities to meet your boss's associates.

Shifting a business relationship to a social one takes lots of patience. But as long as you maintain a level of reserve that is alluring without infringing on the business arrangements, it can be done.

Working as an executive secretary or personal assistant for someone who's wealthy will also give you certain perks. A loyal, hardworking assistant is appreciated by busy executives, and they'll pay to keep you around. You may also be included in some social events, or get invitations to openings and events that your boss can't attend.

Research

If you have skills as a writer, then explore the possibility of doing free-lance journalism. You can meet interesting, professional people while interviewing for articles and networking your way into publication.

Doing research is also one of the best ways to get access to new places. It gives you the ideal excuse to explore new situations and talk to new people. When you go to a golf tournament or an auction for the first time, you can use the experience for the basis of an essay or article.

Even if your article is never published, the process of investigating things with this purpose in mind can give you even more reason tc keep trying.

Volunteer Work

In the Yellow Pages of your telephone directory, you'll find the listings of charities, art galleries, performing arts theaters, historical societies, business associations, and political groups.

Call and put your name on their mailing lists. You'll receive notices of their events and they will usually ask for donations.

Instead of giving money, you can volunteer to help. With charities, you'll mostly meet women, and these contacts can get you entree to other social events.

Working on political campaigns, you can often meet the contributors as well as the candidates and their families.

Historical and art societies usually throw fund-raisers that you can work on. These are specifically aimed at drawing a wealthy crowd.

If you're religious, attend the church or synagogue in the best neighborhoods. These organizations can offer many different opportunities to meet people—in classes and interest groups, choirs, fund-raising efforts, etc. As long as you are involved, you'll be accepted as part of the congregation.

Rehabilitation

If you yourself are a recovering alcoholic, don't forget alcohol or drug rehabilitation clinics. The Alcoholics Anonymous chapter catering to the wealthy part of town can provide a place to meet people without the enticement of alcohol.

They try to make it easy for you to interact with each other because they know that friendly support is the basis of success in any endeavor.

Remember that recovering alcoholics have special needs in their relationships. They are often advised not to get involved in anything serious until they've been living "free" for more than six months. If you aren't sure how to be supportive, the Alcoholics Anonymous chapter will be able to help you.

Read to Be Rich

Even if you can't travel the world, you can experience colorful locales around the world through travel magazines. You can also appreciate the fine homes in *Architectural Digest* magazine, while *Gourmet* will tempt you with the culinary delights of the rich.

The Sunday New York Times

Get a subscription to the Sunday *New York Times* to get a global perspective on the news and events of the day. If you read nothing else but this paper, you'll have more than enough to talk about. To order, you can call 1-800-NYTimes.

Read the entire Arts & Leisure section for the latest on theater, dance, and music from classical to rap, as well as movies, television, architecture, art, and artifacts.

As for the rest of the paper, read:

1. The Front Page, to find out which news is getting priority this week.

2. News Summary on page two. The blurbs will summarize the important stories and give page numbers so you can read more if it sounds interesting.
3. The Editorials/Letters and Op-Ed at the end of the first section. This is a lively section that features outside opinions and comments on the news reported in the *New York Times.*
4. The front page of Business Day (including the Business Digest in the left-hand column). You'll get a quick overview of the world's business news.
5. The Book Review for the latest on literature, biographies, and all the genre fiction you could want.
6. William Safire's column in the *New York Times Magazine.*

Town and Country

Purchase a subscription to *Town and Country.* Sure, this magazine caters to the mature rich woman, but it's the best regular indicator around of the wealthy lifestyle.

Simply the ads will tell point you in the right direction—the best jewelry, cars, vacation sites, etc. The regular departments give you the sophisticated view on money, gardens, beauty, jewelry, clothing design, parties, weddings, and travel.

The magazine features articles on museums, galleries, and interior design, as well as notable social personalities and celebrities. You'll also find little blurbs on things of importance to wealthy people—cellular phones, Palm Beach, new restaurants, and places to go.

5 | *Go Where the Rich Go*

You have to make it happen, so that means doing things differently. You'll have to go into new situations and meet new people—courting uncertainty and failure.

But if there's nothing to be lost, you've got nothing to gain. Avoiding risks simply leaves you right where you are. So if you prefer the safety of familiarity, then you're going to be too busy surviving to actually make bold changes in your life.

Start by going to the most expensive boutiques to window-shop. Eat in the best restaurants, even if you can only have dessert or a salad. Go to the best shows and entertainment—even if it's only once a year. Soak up the atmosphere in art galleries and expensive antique stores, as well as fine furniture showrooms and foreign car dealerships. Put yourself where rich people are, and you will inevitably meet them.

Meanwhile, enjoy yourself—these are the perks of luxury living.

Shopping

Do your shopping in the wealthy neighborhoods. And if you can, shop during off-hours when most working people are busy, such as weekday afternoons.

Take your time, and allow yourself to be seen. People usually return to the same places to shop, and once you've noticed someone interesting, it will be easy to find an opportunity to catch their attention.

Food Stores

Take advantage of gourmet food stores and supermarkets in wealthy areas, and buy something unusual every time you go—a new cheese or flavored coffee.

Enjoy the sensory delight. Who knows? Maybe while lingering over the tea display, you will meet someone interesting.

Specialty Stores

You should also window-shop at the best boutiques and specialty stores. Try on clothes, and get accustomed to the quality and cut. Examine fine luggage, quality furniture, and the high-tech gadgets that make life easier.

Interact with the other customers in the store, using the merchandise to initiate light comments. You never know when a casual acquaintance might turn into a friend, who then introduces you to her friends.

Restaurants

The midday meal can be the best time to eat out. You're less likely to encounter people who are focused on a date.

Go to restaurants that are situated in the business and financial district. If you frequent the same restaurant, the same day every week, then it makes it easier for you to be noticed and approached.

Then, after a few weeks, shake up your routine. Nothing's more exciting than the unexpected.

Inexpensive Restaurants

Coffee shops can be good places to meet people, if they're near a trendy club or nice neighborhood. Go there regularly at odd hours—after midnight or the middle of the afternoon.

Whatever you do, don't waste time and money eating in chain restaurants like steak and seafood places. Save up your money and go to the quality restaurants whenever you go out.

Expensive Restaurants

There are ways to get around the expense in fine dining. You can always eat lunch at the pricier restaurants, which cuts the cost in half. Or you can order a light meal—salad and soup.

As long as your tip corresponds to that of a regular meal, you'll always be treated well.

Tea is another option. It's not as expensive as an evening meal, and it can be a nice treat. But you should go on a weekday afternoon, not the weekend.

One woman told me she and her friend had great success in meeting men at fine restaurants. Since Tess couldn't afford a whole meal, they would go out for dessert around ten or eleven o'clock—the same time the other diners are beginning their dessert. Both women would get up during the meal at least once to go to the bathroom or make a phone call. And they would take their time leaving to give men a chance to approach.

Tess and her friend still got the same excellent service, but only paid a fraction of the price. She also became accustomed to the nicer places in town, and knew exactly where she wanted to go whenever someone asked her out for dinner.

Hotels

Elegant hotels can be a great place to meet people, even if most of the guests will be from out of town. Don't be deterred by this—locals also frequent the fine restaurants in hotels when they come to visit their business associates.

Lobby

When you're walking through the lobby, pause and buy a newspaper or make a phone call. You can even sit down for a few minutes, glancing at your paper, yet staying aware of the people moving through the lobby. Return people's smiles before looking back down, to signal availability.

Bar

Expensive hotels usually have nice bars. Go with a friend, or take work with you—a few folders or a notepad. Then you'll be treated with the respect that a fellow "guest" deserves.

Trendy Spots

Trendy spots are great places to meet people. The problem is, most of us don't find out about the trendy places until they're passe.

You'll have to make friends with the people who make it their priority to know.

To get started, find out which publications cater to the best bars and restaurants in your area. Follow their advice for where to go and when to go there.

Go alone, or with friends, but get out there and meet people.

Performing Arts

Any sort of performing arts event will attract wealthy, cultured people. Get to know the theaters and concert halls in your area. Call and put your name on their mailing lists—you'll be privy to the best entertainment in town.

One thing you can be sure of—anytime there's an opening night, wealthy people will be in attendance. It doesn't matter whether it's a classical concert, opera, ballet, or film festival, always try to attend an opening night.

Fine Art

Even if you don't know anything about art, a gallery or museum is a wonderful place to meet people.

Explore the art galleries in your city. Make sure you put your name on their mailing list every time you go, and you'll receive invitations to their openings.

Art Openings

There will usually be a crowd of people at the opening of a show. Sometimes there are complimentary drinks or wine.

Stop by the front desk and pick up any literature on the artist(s). Glance through it so you have an idea of what the show is about.

Slowly stroll around the entire gallery, looking at each piece. You don't have to linger long over any one of them—just give the entire gallery a once-over. This gives you the chance to give the room the once-over for any interesting-looking people. You allow yourself to see and be seen.

Then return to particular works and take more time examining them. You can work your way toward people, casually chatting, then moving on. Take advantage of the freedom of being able to wander at will, and use it to bring you in contact with other people.

You don't have to act like you know about art. Ask people what they think about certain pieces. Be honest yourself—if you like something, say why. If you think the entire show needs help, then say it. But mostly focus on asking people questions.

Auctions

Auctions, particularly fine art and estate auctions, are often attended by wealthy people. Aside from the dealers who attend, a large percentage of the crowd is made up of private individuals and collectors.

At most auctions, you are free to quietly enter and take a seat to watch the proceedings.

Make sure to ask for a catalog so you can follow the auction, even if you don't register for a paddle. Many people submit written bids, and as far as anyone knows, you're sitting there serenely, waiting for your lot to reach the block.

Bidding

If you want to register to bid, you'll have to produce two pieces of identification and might even have to pay a fee.

You will get a numbered paddle to raise when you want to bid. Each time you flash your paddle, the price is boosted by whatever increment the auctioneer has announced—it could be anywhere from $10 to $10,000, depending on the item.

Sporting Events

Every kind of sport that exists has its share of wealthy patrons.

In stadiums, the best seats are usually reserved for season ticket holders. These are often held by corporations rather than individuals, but the more important the game, the higher the level of executives who will be attending.

When you go to events, try to get into the better seating areas, even if you have to duck around an usher to get there. Usually after halftime, security eases off, and you can slip into one those empty corporate seats that are always available.

You can also wander past the doors to the box seats. Groups of people are usually trying to have a good time in there, and you might be able to join right in.

Tournaments

There are particular tournaments that draw a wealthy audience. Prime examples are sailing races, tennis championships, golf tournaments, and shooting competitions. Attend any sporting event that is hosted by the best clubs in your area.

Golf tournaments are particularly good for providing opportunities to interact freely with the crowd. You can chat as you walk on the course, as long as you keep it short and quiet. Whenever the players are on the course, it's best to watch them instead of trying to make conversation.

Always be the first to move on. And make sure you mingle through the entire crowd, to keep from focusing too much attention on any one person. You may miss someone perfectly marvelous because you got obsessed with the blond you met at the second tee.

After the tournament, there's usually a cocktail party in the clubhouse or pavilion. You may need an invitation or have to buy a ticket to enter, but it's the best place to follow up on anyone interesting you met during the day. Someone may even invite you in as their guest.

Clubs

Yacht clubs draw wealthier members than country clubs, but both are great places to meet people. Call all the clubs in your city and ask about their services and membership fees—that way you'll find out which ones are the most prestigious.

Don't try to get in by acting as if you intend to join. You'll get an extensive sales pitch and will be watched like a hawk while you're being shown around the club.

Instead, call and ask for the club's professional staff— golf, tennis, or sailing instructors. Usually these personal trainers give private lessons to nonmembers at the club facilities.

Taking lessons will give you entry into the club on a regular basis. Ignore the signs that say "Members Only." But don't approach guests or you'll be seen as pushy. You'll be noticed by everyone fast enough simply because you're a new face.

When you enter a group like this, it's best to concentrate on people who are the same sex as you. Make casual comments, then smile and move on. When you do chat with people, focus on the game you're learning. Don't confess you're a rank amateur, but be enthusiastic about practicing more.

Rather than spending your time trying to meet potential mates, your goal should be long-term. Turn acquaintances into practice partners. If you're friendly enough, by the time you finish those lessons, you'll have made friends you can rely on to give you future entry to the club.

Horse Races

Major tracks abound worldwide. More than 60 parimutuel and 380 fair meetings are conducted annually in the United States.

The different types of horse racing attract different spectators, gamblers, and owners. The two main types where you can meet wealthy people are at thoroughbred races and harness races. In fact, harness racing is often held in the evening, and is considered a social event.

Horse racing is a big investment business, and often owners attend the races. They either watch from private rooms or the clubhouse, which is open to everyone. The owner's names are also listed along with the horse.

The best known tracks are New York City's Roosevelt and Yonkers raceways; Hollywood Park in Los Angeles; Sportsman's, Washington; Maywood parks and Hawthorne Race Course in Chicago; and Liberty Bell Park in Philadelphia. Paris has two trotting centers—at Vincennes and Enghein, Rome has Tor di Valle, and Milan has San Siro. Even

Moscow has a track—the Hippodrome. Australia and New Zealand, Austria, Sweden and Germany all have major tracks.

The local newspaper in a track town will cover the horses that are to run the next day. Go to the track and be prepared to learn about racing. Unless you can find something genuinely exciting about it, don't keep going back. People who are passionate about racing will spot your feigned interest a mile away.

Gambling Centers

Many people who gamble are trying to turn a little money into a lot of money. They aren't necessarily rich, and most gamblers aren't even close.

Still, almost all wealthy people enjoy gambling at least once in a while. Some make a regular sport of it, and the hotels are proof of this, with their lavish "high-roller" suites. A high roller is in the mood for having fun, and that's where you come in.

When you go to places where people gamble—Las Vegas, Atlantic City, Monte Carlo—spend your time in only the best casinos. Just ask anyone who works at a casino and they can tell you where to go.

You can always stroll around to see and be seen, but the best way to drag someone's attention from the game to you, is by playing right alongside them.

Baccarat

You'll find the really big money at the baccarat tables. Usually there are security guards posted at the entrance to the room, and you won't be able to go inside unless you intend to play.

Since the players are isolated during the game, you'll have to watch from nearby or pick a slot machine next to the entrance. Make sure you don't become absorbed in your playing. Look around every once in a while, especially as people come and go from the room.

Poker

You might as well avoid the poker tables. The games can be high stakes, but the players don't talk to anybody. You can also make people nervous if you stand around watching.

Blackjack

Blackjack doesn't offer much opportunity to interact with the other players. When you're at a table, everyone can hear what you say.

But if you see someone you'd like to meet playing blackjack, it's easy to slip into a game and play a few hands. At the very least, you can make eye contact before moving on again.

Playing blackjack is simple. Bet the minimum amount for the table. Hold at anything above sixteen. You may not always win, but you'll look like you know what you're doing if you don't dither around.

Roulette

Roulette is a popular game among high rollers, and there's plenty of opportunity for interaction around the table. This game is more popular in Europe than in America, so there's a slightly sophisticated air that comes with playing roulette.

Roulette consists of a table and a wheel. The table has thirty-six numbered rectangular spaces, colored red and black alternately, arranged in three columns. At the bottom of each column are spaces marked first 12, second 12, and third 12.

The dealer will call for you to place your bets. You can put a chip directly on a number, or on a line or intersection of lines to bet on more than one number. You can put chips in as many places as you wish, but it's best to stick to one or two.

A low-odds bet is to place your chip at the bottom of a column to cover twelve numbers at once. There are also low-number, high-number spaces, in which the chips are placed on the space marked 1-18 (manque) or on the space marked 19-36 (passe): payoff is even money. Or you can place a chip on red (rouge) or black (noir), or on the odd-number, even-number spaces.

The dealer spins the wheel, and bets may be made until he calls, "No more bets!"

The ball will come to rest on a number of the wheel, and the dealer will announce the winning numbers, and the winning color. The dealer will first collect the losing bets, leaving the chips on the winning number. Then he will pay off the winning spaces.

Craps

Craps also attracts high rollers and is a very good place to interact with other people.

The two dice are thrown by the shooter, and the numbers are added together. The basics of craps goes like this: on the first throw, a natural (7 or 11) is called a pass—a winner. The shooter can roll again. If it is a crap (2, 3, or 12) it's a missout—a loser. Then the dice are passed to the next person. If the numbers add up to 4, 5, 6, 8, 9, or 10, that number becomes the point and the shooter continues to throw the dice until he either throws the point again (considered a pass—a winner) or throws a 7 (a missout—a loser).

The table is covered with a "craps layout" divided into spaces representing the various bets that can be placed. You can place your bet anytime before the throw. You can bet that the first throw will be a pass (7 or 11) or a crap (2, 3 or 12), or a certain number (the odds are higher against this).

You don't have to bet every roll, and if the table isn't crowded, nobody will think twice if you stand there even if you only bet occasionally.

If the dice are handed to you, you have the option of passing them on if you wish. But do yourself a favor and take advantage of being the center of attention.

One man realized the wisdom of this advice when he went ahead and took his place as shooter. Stephen got on a roll, throwing six passes in a row, which stirred the excitement at his table. Later, one of the women who'd been playing took the opportunity to come up to him and comment on his "technique."

Parties

Who says you have to wait for an invitation to go to a party? Hotels, bars, restaurants, and clubs throw private parties all the time, and if you stand on ceremony, you're missing out on the fun.

It's remarkably easy to crash parties and get into ticketed events. Even if you're caught, the worst that can happen is that you're asked to leave. As long as you acquiesce, there won't be any fuss made.

Usually, you'll have to be spontaneous when you run across a party. You can also go to the better establishments and get to know the service people—they can tell you about parties that are coming up.

Make sure it's a large enough party so that you'll blend in. Don't try to crash dinner parties or intimate gatherings.

Getting Inside

Wait until the party is in full swing before you enter. If there is a hallway or restroom outside the party, then go there as soon as you arrive. From there, you can judge the best time to try to get past the invitation or ticket taker. Wait until there are several people at the door, trying to get in. Most of the time, you can skim past without even being noticed.

It's important to act as if you've already been inside. If there's a crowd at the door, avoid looking at anyone as you walk in. If you're alone, smile and nod briefly to the person taking invitations, then quickly slide your eyes to the room as if looking for someone. Don't stop, keep right on walking. If you are stopped, say, "I came in earlier." If you know someone who could have been invited, mention their name. Then keep on walking.

You can also tell the invitation taker that you need to speak with someone for a moment. Don't wait for a response. Say "thank you" as if you're certain they'll give in to such a simple request. You can even say, "There she is," as if you see your friend—as you walk in.

If you're stopped again, then quietly give in to the inevitable and leave.

Once You're Inside

Once you've made it inside, you belong there. There's no need to slink around, trying to avoid the host. There are so many friends of friends and their dates that nobody's keeping track.

You probably will be noticed as a new face, but use that to your advantage. People will also ask who you know at the party, trying to find something in common with you.

Don't react as if they're interrogating you. The smoothest answer is "a friend of a friend" of the host—"I came with a friend of Jerry's." Even if you're talking to the best friend of the host, they won't know everyone who was invited, and "Jerry" could be anyone. Don't give them time to think about it—immediately ask who is their connection to the host. Then casually keep on asking questions, focusing the conversation on them.

Don't talk to any one person for too long. And be the first to move on. You're at the party to meet as many people as possible.

When you crash, it's particularly important to cultivate the people of your own sex. If you're only flirting with the opposite sex, you're bound to raise hackles on everyone who was invited.

6 | *Etiquette for the 21st Century*

Good manners are the grease that eases the wheels of interaction. The basic rules of polite behavior can help guide you in how you conduct yourself.

Not that rules of etiquette are intended to be a strait jacket, but they are the standard from which you can deviate in order to make your own personal statement.

For example, if you're at a dinner party and you sit down in the chair from the right instead of the left, it's likely no one will notice, much less care. But as Letitia Baldrige says in *Amy Vanderbilt's Everyday Etiquette*: "If we think we're 'doing the right thing' we walk with more ease, we feel better about ourselves, and we interact far more humanely with our fellow men and women."

So if you understand conventional decorum, you won't feel yourself at a loss in any situation.

Style

Style is sometimes described as grace under pressure. It is the art of maintaining a sense of control even when the situation is unusual or unpleasant.

Basic good manners are essential to maintaining a successful style. Be polite, considerate, and unassuming—these are the foundation of good manners. And as long as you respect the feelings of other people, you can interact with anyone with style.

Embarrassing Incidents

Why is it that an embarrassing moment can sometimes be the worst thing to endure? It can be the reason we avoid new things—because we aren't sure we'll do it right.

That's because being different from others is rooted in our sense of survival. After tens of thousands of generations of evolution, our instincts tell us that when we deviate from the pack, we are in danger.

The best thing to do when something awkward happens is to make the least amount of fuss possible. If you break something, quietly offer to replace it, then follow it up at a later time. If you mistake a woman's husband for her father, serenely ignore it and move on.

The less you react, the quicker others—and you—will forget the incident. After all, most of our embarrassing memories are actually rather stupid and trivial.

Disagreements

When you're in a social situation, it's expected that you will express a differing opinion during discussions. But don't let it get serious.

It doesn't matter if the subject is one you've dedicated your life's blood to upholding—if you want to have a serious discussion, make sure you're in the setting to do so. Social occasions are not the setting.

If you see that something can't be discussed in a pleasant manner, ask the other person to go someplace private where you can talk, or defer the matter to another time. A public debate will only serve to make everyone else feel uncomfortable.

If someone tries to argue with you, politely tell them this isn't the time or place to discuss the matter. You aren't obligated to defend yourself or your point. In a situation like this, nobody cares who's right or wrong—but they will always remember who was involved in an ugly scene.

If someone is being offensive, it's best not to say anything. Simply excuse yourself and move away.

Some Simple Old-Fashioned Rules

Don't indulge in crude jokes or quips, even if others are.

Don't chew gum in public.

Don't smoke on the street or in someone's home, unless they do so first.

Always say "thank you" when someone helps you or gives you something. Always say "pardon me" when passing someone.

There are also still rules of etiquette that reflect the traditional gender stereotypes. For instance, men usually help women with putting on their coats, but a woman can also graciously lend a hand for her date.

Crossing Rooms

When you're crossing a room with your date, who goes first? Usually, the man goes first, with the woman following.

On the other hand, if an usher or waiter is leading a couple through a room, the man will typically follow the woman.

Stairs

Men should walk upstairs behind a woman, and walk downstairs in front of a woman. This is practical advice—women in high heels have a particularly hard time going downstairs, and it helps to have someone in front.

Also, it's nice for men to turn at the bottom, and offer a hand to help her descend the last few steps.

Automobiles

When you're in a limousine, always wait for the chauffeur to open the door for you.

Otherwise, men do still open car doors for their dates. You don't have to make a point of it—be smooth and unobtrusive with your help. But unless you're in formal wear, women don't need to make a point of sitting there waiting.

It's also nice for a man to offer to assist his date from the car by simply holding out a hand. Don't pull, but hold firm, letting your date lean on you as she gets out. If she doesn't take your hand, step back immediately so you're not in her way. It may simply be a combination of dress and heels that make it easier for her to get out herself.

When you enter a car, don't go in headfirst. Bending and stepping at the same time makes your body look awkward. Instead, sit on the edge of the seat and swing your legs together inside. This works particularly well for women in high heels. If you enter a car this way consistently, it can become a graceful, natural act.

Introductions

When you introduce yourself, clarity is the key point. Look the other person in the eye, and state your first and last name. Repeat their name after them to make sure you've heard it correctly.

There are many ways to respond to an introduction, but you'll always be safe with, "Nice to meet you." It makes more sense and sounds less pretentious than "How do you do?"

When a friend approaches two or more people who are talking, they should be introduced to everyone else immediately. If your date neglects to introduce you, by all means, introduce yourself. That way, they won't forget next time.

Handshake

If the setting is more formal or professional, then both men and women should extend their hands. If the situation is casual, it's acceptable to meet people with a simple nod of your head.

But if you want to make real contact, always offer your hand when you meet someone new. It serves as a marker of the introduction, and it will give you a few moments to imprint their name and their face in your memory.

Stand

It also makes more of an impact when you stand while being introduced—this is true for both men and women. The common rule is that men should stand for an introduction, while women can remain seated. However, equality is equality.

If you're greeting someone you know, you can remain seated even if you shake hands or kiss.

Order of Introduction

Usually, the person of lesser importance is introduced to the more prominent person. "Senator Joseph, may I introduce Lily Carr." Or in the way a child is introduced to an adult—"Billy, this is Aunt Josephine."

It can be a subtle indicator of someone's attitude when they are introducing you.

When two people are officially a couple (either living together or married), and an introduction needs to be made to a third party, then the stranger is introduced to your mate.

Remembering Names

There are some easy mnemonic devices you can use to aid your memory. For instance, if a man's name is Pete, remember that it rhymes with "eat"—especially if Pete is slightly rounding in the middle. Or if you meet a blond woman who's name is Marilyn—you can associate the blond hair with Marilyn Monroe. No matter what the woman really looks like, the sight of her blond hair will make you remember Marilyn.

What if you need to introduce someone and you've forgotten their name? Simply say the name of the person you do know, explaining your connection with the person who's name you've forgotten. If you give enough information nobody will notice you didn't include a name.

For instance, if you're with a date and you're trying to introduce a woman whose name you can't remember, you can say—"Perry, this is that friend of Joe's I was telling you about that grows tulips. We met at that party—what was it three, weeks ago? I think it was at your brother's house."

Very likely, Perry will shake the woman's hand and you all will continue the conversation in that vein without realizing you've never said her name. At some point, Perry will probably ask for her name. Don't catch your "mistake," but simply smile and imprint that name on your mind so it doesn't happen again.

If you misstate someone's name, quietly say "Excuse me," and continue the introductions. People usually don't mind as long as you don't make a big deal of it.

7 | *Table Manners*

Good table manners are one of the last bastions of sophistication. They can often be used as a litmus test of your upbringing.

Whether you're in a restaurant or someone's home, your table manners need to be impeccable.

Basics

Don't sneeze at the table, and at least turn away if you don't have time to get up. Cover your mouth and nose with a napkin and immediately excuse yourself. Go to the bathroom to blow your nose, never do it at the table.

If you burp or hiccough, cover your mouth with your napkin, and say (to no one in particular) "Excuse me."

Don't use your fingernails or utensils to dislodge food stuck in your teeth.

And never smoke at the table until the dessert is finished and the coffee is being served. Only smoke if the host(s) does. Don't ever ask first.

Food

When you're in a restaurant, the proper way to share food is before anyone has taken a bite. Section off samples of your meal and slide them onto the other person' s plate. Then you can start eating.

When you're at a dinner party, follow the lead of the host or hostess. Especially if something tricky is served, like artichokes, lobster, or asparagus.

Other things to.remember:

- Use your napkin before sipping your drink.
- Never butter an entire piece of bread. Break off a bite-sized piece and butter that before you eat it.
- Don't put salt or pepper on your food before you've tasted it.

Service

You will be served from the left, and dishes will be removed from your right. If speed is desired, plates will be removed simultaneously from two diners.

A place plate or "charger" is larger than a dinner plate and is on the table when you sit down. It is used for decoration and to hold smaller plates and bowls. It is usually removed permanently from the table at the end of the first course.

Bread plates are becoming a thing of the past. Place your bread on the upper left side of your plate. It's also acceptable to place your bread on the tablecloth to the left of the table setting—but this isn't really the most refined thing to do.

Never put your napkin on the table until you get up to leave. Even if everyone's lingering long over coffee while you've refused a cup, keep your napkin on your lap.

A stemmed water or wine goblet is held at its base with your thumb and two fingers. Chilled wine glasses should be held by the stem just beneath the base.

A polite way to refuse more wine is to touch the rim of your wineglass as the waiter approaches with the bottle. Usually you don't have to shake your head, the gesture is warning enough.

Silverware

Don't worry too much about the silverware. Usually the correct silver is placed for the course that is being presented, and the unnecessary pieces are removed. If you have more than one choice, use the utensil on the outside first.

When not in use:

The butter knife is placed across the top of the plate, the blade toward the user.

Always rest a spoon not in use on the underplate or saucer of anything you're eating or sipping it with—coffee spoon on saucer, the soup spoon on your plate.

When you're done, place your knife and fork side by side in the middle of your plate. The fork tines should be down, with the knife to its right, with the sharp blade pointing inward toward the fork.

Leaving the table

When you leave the table during the meal, place your napkin on the table to the left of your place setting, not on your chair. If you sit down again, immediately return the napkin to your lap.

Men are supposed to rise when a woman joins their table, or at least make a motion of rising out of courtesy. Women should seat themselves quickly rather than forcing men to a full stand.

Restaurants

When you take someone to a nice restaurant, always make reservations. It's not necessary to tip the maitre d' in advance, although it's fairly common in the pricier restaurants.

How long do you wait at a restaurant if someone's late? You can call their home or office if they're twenty minutes late, and at thirty minutes, you should leave.

The host should offer their guests the best seats that face the restaurant.

Service

Restaurant employees are there to serve you. They know what they're doing, and they're ready to help you. Pay attention to the waiter and the maitre d', they will offer you choices to make everything flow smoothly—from pointing out the correct silverware to use, to offering you an aperitif after dinner.

After you are taken to your table, stand to the left of the chair and allow the waiter or maitre d' to pull it out for you. Sit down briefly, then lift up to allow them to scoot the chair under you.

Immediately pick up your napkin and unfold it across your lap, unless the waiter does it for you.

Don't tip less than 20 percent. There are a lot of people to take care of: the maitre d', captain, wine steward, headwaiter, and waiter.

Protocol

It isn't necessary for a man to order for a woman, but it is more traditional. In the finer restaurants, it can create a certain atmosphere, even a feeling of intimacy, when the man orders the dinner. For a woman, unless your date asks what you would like, assume you're ordering for yourself.

When getting up from the table, it's not necessary for the man to assist the woman from her chair. However, if you have risen first and there is the opportunity, it can be a gracious way to end the meal.

If an acquaintance approaches your table, stop eating. For men, it's more polite to stand until the acquaintance leaves—it marks a separation between your private meal and your interaction with the outer world.

8 | *Being a Guest*

When you're a guest, you're obligated to adhere to the customs of your host. For example, if grace is said at the table, you should join in no matter what your denomination or religious beliefs are.

Smoking preferences should also be respected. Don't ask your host if you can smoke unless there are ashtrays clearly provided.

What to Wear

Is it better to overdress or underdress? If you're not sure, the best choice is something more casual than your original impulse.

People usually make the mistake of overdressing. Wearing a suit to a tennis tournament or an evening dress to a dinner party reveals that too much effort is being made for the occasion. Clothes which are simple yet refined will always be acceptable.

The one time when dressing down is a mistake is when you go to a black-tie affair. Always dress formally for these occasions. If you weren't aware that it was to be a formal event and you arrive without being dressed appropriately, it's best to apologize quietly to your hosts, then ignore it. If anyone mentions it, laugh it off.

If you're truly uncomfortable—appearing in jeans at a

wedding reception—go home and change. Do return, and mention nothing about your transformation, or it will look like you've run away with your tail between your legs.

Discussing Clothing Choice

If you know the host or hostess, it's permissible to call and ask how "everyone" will be dressed. They will tell you what they're going to wear, and you can follow suit.

Don't discuss your clothing choice with your escort. It shows that you're uncertain of yourself. Do ask what the event is and where it's being held—that should give you enough of a clue to make your own choice.

Private Parties

Find out the names of your host and hostess from your escort and *remember* them.

If someone other than the host or hostess answers the door, give your name and state the event you are attending. Have your invitation in a pocket or your purse, rather than in your hand.

It's up to you to find and greet your host or hostess if they aren't near at hand. But don't try to catch up on things right then—keep it short. They have a million things on their minds and many people to see, and this isn't the time to get into a discussion about *anything*.

A polite host will usually point you in the next direction, offering the bar or indicating a particular group of people you might want to see. They might even offer introductions to some friends, which you should accept graciously.

Before you leave, make sure you seek out your host to say thank you and goodbye. Again, make it short, but compliment some aspect of the event that particularly appealed to you. People like it when their carefully arranged details are noticed and appreciated.

Dinner Parties

When you're invited to dinner at eight o'clock, when should you arrive? From eight until eight-thirty is polite.

Definitely don't arrive a minute before eight—early is not the same as prompt, and will be viewed with almost as much displeasure by a harried host as someone who is an hour late.

If you are detained, call your host and urge them to go ahead and serve dinner on time. *Briefly*, explain the urgent reasons you are detained—remember that your host's mind will be on their party—and tell them the exact time you will arrive.

Even if you're in a hurry, don't leave a dinner party right after the coffee has been served. Usually, it's polite to wait fifteen minutes to half an hour after coffee service. Everyone should leave within an hour after coffee is served, unless there is dancing or some sort of entertainment planned for the rest of the evening.

Seating Arrangements

Quite often you can tell the relative importance of the guests according to the seating arrangement. If the host and hostess are seated at the ends of the table, usually the guests of honor are seated to their right.

Sometimes, the female guest of honor is seated at the end opposite the hostess. This usually places the host to her right, and the male guest of honor to the right of the hostess.

People take their own seats at the table. Traditional men may still assist the lady on their right into her seat.

Do wait until the hostess sits before you sit down.

Service

The main course will usually be presented to you on a platter. The waiter often encourages you to take a serving of the vegetable or garniture around the meat.

If you are served lots of little things on a platter—birds, small lamb chops, slices of meat—the safest bet is to take only one. The platter will always be passed again.

If you drop the serving utensils or arrange them awkwardly, allow the waiter to rearrange them. It's their job, and you'll look more poised if you turn away immediately.

At a buffet dinner, you may sit down while everyone else is serving themselves. Also, begin eating as soon as you have your food.

Formal Dinner Party

A formal dinner party will be announced with engraved invitations and a request for formal evening dress or black tie.

Often, a chef has prepared the meal, and formally dressed waiters will do the serving (one to every six guests). Four or five courses will be served, along with two or more wines.

The tablecloth and napkins will be the finest linen, and the table service fine china, silver, and crystal. Sometimes there are place cards at each setting, or a seating chart that the butler will show you.

Weekend Guest

Ask your escort what sort of activities are expected. It could include anything from a formal dinner one night, followed by a dance at a club, to an informal swim party.

Usually your host or hostess will provide the exact time of your expected arrival and departure. Arrive on time and leave on time, don't allow yourself to be "talked into" staying an extra day.

Being a guest means you have certain responsibilities, including:

- Bring a tasteful present—wine, flowers, or
  something more personal if you know them well.

Or send a present afterward, if you prefer.
- Never bring other guests, children, or pets who weren't specifically invited.
- Never go to someone's home when you're sick.
- Keep your own room neat, even if there is a maid. Offer to help occasionally, but don't be overbearing about it.
- Participate in the organized activities. Nobody likes a party pooper.
- If you break something, immediately tell your host that you intend to replace the item. Then no matter what their objections are, make sure you replace it.

Travel

Purchase a nice piece of luggage that could hold your effects for a weekend. Don't ever bring more than two bags.

When you're traveling, it's best to bring only one bag into the cabin with you and check everything else. That keeps you from crowding your seat mates.

Also, make sure your passport is in order so you're always prepared for spontaneous trips.

9 | *Developing a Relationship*

Once you've made contact with someone, developing a relationship will take effort on your part. But there are certain kinds of behavior that facilitate the growth of intimacy.

In particular, there are certain things to consider when you're dealing with successful people. They are usually accustomed to being watched and talked about, and their behavior can be more circumspect because of that. It can take time to get past the social façade that keeps the rest of the crowd at a distance.

Wealthy people are also well aware of the effect that power and money has on other people. If they're rich enough, they're used to friends and strangers flocking around them because of their money. They've seen it do both good and bad things to people's values and personalities, and they will probably be wary of your reaction.

Even if they take a certain ego-satisfaction from seeing your eyes light up with admiring interest at the mention of their house in Malibu or their yacht in St. Petersburg, it doesn't earn their respect.

So what do wealthy people respect?

They certainly respect other people who are rich. But they also know that hard work is the key to success, not luck or money.

Anyone who is striving to progress and struggling to improve themselves will be admired.

Listen

The best way to develop a relationship is by listening to someone. Always pursue the things that people talk about by asking more questions.

That seems to go without saying, doesn't it? But often when you start to develop a rapport with someone, you're tempted to tell them everything about your own dreams and desires. But that makes it easy to fall into an illusion about a relationship—because you're the only one building it.

Don't ever let the impulse to create intimacy interfere with the natural growth and development of your relationship. Get control of your interest in someone, and take your time to get to know them—only then will your interest lead to love.

Be Yourself

Don't try to look or act like anyone else. You have to be an individual in order to stand out from the crowd.

When you alter your behavior or appearance to "fit in" better, you're letting your fear and insecurities take over. You'll never get anywhere if you spend all of your time reacting to the situation around you.

Truly successful people don't copy anyone—they're out there on the cutting edge. They're self-reliant and resourceful. They make the most of every experience and they appreciate others who do, as well.

Be honest with yourself. That comes first. Then if you really want to be unique, be honest with other people.

Be Positive

The way you approach new situations is very revealing. If you are unsure of yourself, wary or fearful, you won't get much out of the experience. If you are willing to learn, by showing how much you don't know, then you'll be able to fully experience things.

Don't ever complain about being bored or lonely. It's an immediate turn-off, even if you aren't interested in someone as a potential mate.

Your negative emotions will also block you from taking opportunities. When you're cynical, or doubtful, or merely too wrapped up in yourself to see what's right in front of your eyes, you're missing out on life.

Be Diplomatic

Praise the good points in other people—both men and women. If you start thinking of someone in terms of "competition" then others will, too.

Don't ever talk negatively about other people, even if someone else does. Sometimes misunderstandings keep people apart, when all it takes is stepping back from the situation. Today's enemy may be tomorrow's ally if you don't burn your bridges.

For example, Danny was dating a wealthy woman who was fighting with her best friend. He thought he could speed their intimacy by taking his lover's side in the argument, and agreeing with her opinions of her friend. Unfortunately, this backfired when the two women resolved their differences, while Danny continued to criticize his lover's oldest friend. Soon, she ended the relationship.

Remember that the goodwill you create will help people trust you—that's your social safety net.

Pleasing

If you want to be remembered, you'll have to be a challenge. Don't make the mistake of trying to please the people you're most interested in.

Wealthy people are used to being stroked and admired—it's one of the consequences of having money. In the same way, celebrities usually have hordes of people fawning over them.

If you think you're going to win someone over by doing everything they want, you're quite mistaken. It's the quickest way to end up in the type of relationship *they* want, instead of the one you want.

Intimidation

Don't make the mistake of being too easily impressed by other people's jobs or possessions or vacations.

It's almost impossible to rise from the "groupie" crowd once you've asked for an autograph or gushed over someone's Mazerati. It immediately puts you in different spheres of life.

Instead, find the unusual or incongruous in situations, when you make light comments. Don't criticize—it's not your opinion that's important, but the things you notice. Maybe it's an exotic food or unusual piece of art or the fact that everyone in the room is wearing black.

Be Elusive

Since love grows fastest when we're giving and investing in someone—why not let someone give and invest in you?

After all, people typically end up wanting the things they can't have. Use that to your advantage in the beginning of a relationship to heat up someone else's interest.

Giving Out Your Phone Number

Whenever someone asks for your number, your initial response—even if you're interested in that person—should be to hesitate.

Make them work for it. After all, you don't just give your number to anyone who asks.

You could even ask for their number instead, which leaves the ball in your hands. With people you aren't sure about, this is always the best bet.

Be Discreet

When you're becoming part of a crowd, don't let everyone know your personal business.

For instance, Debbie got into a wealthy crowd through her cousin's husband. She knew she wanted marriage, and fully intended to get a wealthy man. Her mistake was talking about it with her cousin's husband. It wasn't long before the whole circle of friends had labeled her as a gold-digger, even if it was mostly a joke. She says now that it was that perception of her that interfered the most with meeting people.

It's enough to let your potential mates know what sort of relationship you would like through your preferences and actions.

Availability

Don't make the mistake of being too available. Sure you have to make enough time to develop the relationship, but you shouldn't let it disrupt the rest of your life.

Never compromise work or break other engagements to be with a potential mate. That places too much emphasis on this goal and weights each encounter with too much significance.

Take Your Time

Give people a chance to *want* to know you. That will make your thoughts and feelings all the more important to them. This doesn't mean playing hard to get—but don't give yourself away lightly, either.

It's fine to be interested in someone, but be circumspect about giving away your love. Make potential mates prove their sincerity. That takes time. No amount of money or assurances can replace that.

You can date someone, enjoy spending time together, even have wonderful sex together, but that shouldn't make you ready to throw yourself at their feet. That sort of enthusiasm can seem desperate, and sometimes even the smallest hint of eagerness can be a turn-off.

Develop Other Relationships

It's very important that dating doesn't become your sole social outlet. Develop relationships with people who aren't potential mates.

Getting to know someone brings you into their life—and that gives you opportunities to meet new people. You never know what that might bring.

One man learned how important it was to pursue every friendly opportunity—Karl met a woman whom he wasn't attracted to, but he knew she loved dancing. While ballroom dancing with her, Karl met his future wife.

The more social options you have, the more control you have over your own life. And it will keep you from focusing too much on new relationships that do have the potential to lead to commitment.

Make Friends

When you meet someone, explore their possibilities.
Find out what you might enjoy doing together. If you like

sailing, and they like sailing, go sailing even if you're sure you're never going to marry that person.

Make the most of everyone who comes into your life—it's not cynical or mercenary as long as you don't mislead someone about your affections.

Friends are people who do things together and support each other. It's a mutual relationship that benefits everyone.

10 | *The Art of Pursuing Someone*

The best way to move a relationship along is by being friendly and casual. If the other person seems receptive, you can mention lectures and events that may appeal to them. Or you can suggest that you both to go to a show at the theater or an art gallery.

Whatever you do, don't pay too much attention to the people you're interested in. They'll instinctively react in a defensive way, closing themselves off to you. When you're giving them all that free attention, they don't need to make any effort.

Once you do catch their attention, accept their interest as if it's your natural due. Let them pursue you.

Rejection

If someone doesn't respond to your casual comments, or barely returns your hello, don't take it personally—even though it might be difficult to remember in the heat of the moment.

We all have a strong desire for other people' s approval—the "tribal" instinct dictated by the need for human beings to band together just to survive. Call it a primitive response to something that has become much more complex.

Consider Their Situation

Often what you consider to be rejection isn't that at all. It's usually temporary, born of that moment and situation.

Usually, people don't think outwardly. They're concerned with their own problems and needs.

For example, Charlotte became upset once when she greeted a man she was interested in, and he turned away without a word. The next time she saw him, though he acted very pleasant, she responded coldly. It was only later she found out that all of his friends knew he'd been going through a hard time with a serious illness in his family. It was too late for Charlotte, though—she was never able to revive his interest.

Remember that while today you may not be noticed, tomorrow that same person could fall in love at "first" sight, simply because their situation is different.

React Casually

If you do take everything personally, you're not going to be able to interact casually. To be a successful networker, you must learn how to be adept at pleasant, casual encounters.

By serenely moving on as if it doesn't matter—which it doesn't—you make the encounter unimportant. That's all that matters.

Then the next time you see that person, your emotions will be unruffled when you greet them.

Be Discreet

When you're interested in someone, don't tell anyone. Let your relationship grow before you start hashing it over with your best friend—otherwise you're speculating on dreams.

Telling Friends

If you must discuss it, pick someone who doesn't know

your potential mate. When you tell friends and acquaintances, it affects their attitude even if they manage to keep
your secret.

Usually friends give you away, intending to "help you."
However subtle they try to be, they end up destroying any
leverage you might have.

Telling Their Friends

Never, ever hint or suggest that you are interested in
someone's friend. Don't make the mistake of thinking that's
the quickest way to get access to your potential mate.

You'll never be able to interact naturally while you're in a
fishbowl with all of their friends watching. You may even
meet resistance or disastrously "helpful" attempts to force
you two together.

Besides, most people feel as if they're being stalked if
rumors of your interest reach them before you do. Keep your
private feelings to yourself, where they belong.

One example shows how successful you can be this way.
A few years ago, Michael saw a woman on a local fund-
raising show and decided he wanted to get to know her. He
began to volunteer for that organization, and was friendly
with her friends. He became one of the group without
letting anyone know the real reason he was there.

He gradually won her interest, and only after six months
into their dating relationship did he admit the way he'd
tracked her down. By then, she was thrilled to find out he'd
gone to such trouble.

With a little private dedication, he got exactly the woman
he wanted.

Create Encounters

If you want to get to know someone, you can make it

happen. But it's also true that being too overt can repel or frighten people off.

Get to Know Their Friends

When you see someone interesting, take a moment and note who they're with.

Then take any opportunity you can to talk to those people—be casual and friendly, but establish some sort of connection before you move on. Either introduce yourself on some sort of pretext, or simply comment on something you have in common (the party, the food, etc).

Later on, you'll have an excuse for speaking with them again—when they're with the person you're really interested in.

Join in Conversations

If you want to meet someone who's always with other people, don't let that stop you. Join right in.

Don't make the mistake of directly approaching that person. Talk to their friends instead.

If you approach someone who's with a date, make their date your primary focus. Otherwise it will seem like you're trying to horn in. At the most, during the course of a casual exchange, introduce yourself to the person you're really interested in.

Run Into Them

Deliberately put yourself in the path of people you like. If they live next to a park, then make it your habit to go to the park. If they frequent a certain restaurant, then eat in that restaurant.

Once you know where someone works or lives, you can arrange casual encounters there. But make sure weeks pass in between, otherwise your intentions will be too transparent.

One woman even admitted that she tried a strategy she read about. When a man didn't respond to her initial overtures, Annette called and left a "wrong" message on his answering machine. She pretended that she had to break a date, and her message conveyed the fact that she was both socially desirable and conscientious. But she didn't leave her number. A week later, she left another message, this time cajoling him to "not be mad. I'll make it up to you... only it's best if we just stay friends." This time she left her number.

Annette got a call back that night informing her that she had called the "wrong" number. The man was so intrigued that she was even able to parley the conversation into a dinner invitation.

11 | *Make an Impact*

Sometimes, you've only got a few seconds to make an impact. Before you wear out your welcome making unsuccessful overtures, you'd better make sure you hit on something that's important to the person you're interested in.

Friends

You can find out the most useful information from people's friends. Not only will you find out about the person you're interested in, but you'll get to know the kind of people around him or her.

You can also watch someone interact with their friends. Then you'll be able to see how they treat other people.

One of the quickest ways to determine who is rich is by watching them with others. Men in particular will compete with and/or defer to other men who have more power and wealth. No matter what the conversation is about, the more powerful people will be watched by the others.

Questions to Ask

Ask about someone's association with the person you're interested in. Pursue that subject by talking about their involvement.

Ask about the other things their friend has achieved.

What do they focus on—business? Creative pursuits? Ethical and social concerns?

Find people who are old friends or get to know their family. That way you can find out where someone grew up, and where they've lived in the past. Listen for patterns in their past relationships, and find out the true state of their availability.

How to Ask

Remember—above all else—be casual when you're asking questions.

Don't make the mistake of asking about only one person in particular. Ask about other people, first. And let free association fill in the background information—talking about other people in their friend's past.

Spread your questions among the various members of the social group. Not only will that keep you from focusing too much on one person, but others won't have a chance to pick up on your secret obsession.

Listen to Criticisms

Whenever people say something critical about their friends, they're pointing out something that is very important to the person you're interested in—something they spend too much time or money on.

Sonya learned the value of this after she met her future husband. He didn't seem interested in her at first, but then she heard a friend exclaiming over the way he had shipped a horse to Virginia for his vacation, she knew she had her man. Sonya was a good western rider, and could talk horses with the best. She also made a point of furthering her own skill by taking a few lessons in English riding.

Sonya soon caught her husband's attention by mentioning her riding. In his mind, he equated her with something he valued, and that was all it took to start their relationship off right.

Money

Practicalities aside, we all tend to spend our money emotionally. That's why advertising has become such a big business—preferences can be swayed by appealing to our ego and insecurities, or by tugging on our heartstrings.

You can learn a lot about someone by watching the way they spend money.

Image

People use their money to create a certain image of themselves. This image can tell you what they value the most.

Maybe they're flamboyant, picking up the tab when it makes a statement. Or do they want to appear wealthier than they are?

Some people try to appear more cultured than everyone else, while others date extravagant young women to prove their status.

If you see signs like this, then presenting yourself as an asset to someone's status might be the best approach.

Spending Habits

Some people say you can tell how people will treat you by the way they spend their money. If a man is careful with money, he'll be careful with relationships. If a woman is careless with cash, then she will be careless with her lovers.

Watch to see whether someone prefers quality or quantity. You can appeal to their discerning taste by appreciating objects that are rare and prized, and by presenting yourself as something unique, as well.

On the other hand, if someone pays to fly to parties and

constant excitement is what they crave, you can be appreciated for always keeping things fun.

What if someone is generous, without wanting any attention to be made to their contributions? They may be looking
for appreciation of a different sort—for themselves instead
of their money.

Then again, some people are tight—ever watchful for
what they're getting, or afraid of being "taken." Then it's
likely they'll be equally watchful of your actions in the
relationship.

Money Management

Listen to how people talk about their finances. Is it all
show? What are they doing now? Do they talk about big
deals and future income, but do nothing to make it happen?

If they depend on credit or have a bankruptcy in their
past, it could be they have a different idea of permanency
than you do.

It's true that economic reasons can force a company to file
bankruptcy, but the way someone reacts to that failure can
be telling. Are they living on remnants of past success? Do
they blame the economy, or insist that they had nothing to
do with the mismanagement?

Deferring responsibility when it comes to money is a
fairly good indicator that the word "responsibility" doesn't
mean much. After all, they left creditors holding the bag—
people and companies who believed in them. What's to
keep them from doing it to you?

But if they honestly admit to a failed business, and
they're using the knowledge gained to rebuild their life—
you've got someone who knows the meaning of money and
stability. They can appreciate what they have.

Research

It's easy to do research to find out more about someone you're interested in. Even if all you have is their name, you can find out things from their personal achievements to their income level.

For example, if you're wondering whether a person has money, there are certain things you can look for:

- the location of their residence
- attendance in private schools or Ivy League colleges
- owning or founding a business
- being a donor to charities and the arts
- being on the board of a foundation
- memberships in exclusive clubs

City Directory

The first place to look is in the city directory. You can find it in your local library.

The city directory is a cross-reference of everyone who lives in your area. You can look up an address and find out who lives there, or you can look up the name of someone and find out where they live. If you know the phone number, you can find out both names and addresses.

The city directory also includes spouses and other residents. Sometimes you can even find out what someone's occupation is or the name of their principle business in the directory.

Index Section

The library has a vast reference section that includes indexes of magazine articles by subject, author and date. You can also access microfiche copies of your local newspaper.

If the task of tracking someone down seems daunting, your librarian can set you on the right path in only a few minutes. You can look up someone's name (if they're prominent), their company, or even special interests they're involved in.

For example, one man found out that a woman was a docent at the local museum. Since Karl couldn't dedicate a few hours a week volunteering, he went to the library and looked up recent articles that made reference to the museum. He discovered that there was a several-year battle going on over the amount of funding the museum received.

After that, it was easy for Karl to casually ask the woman's opinion on the subject, creating a conversation that truly caught her attention.

New York Times

Aside from your local newspaper, you can also access references to people in the index for the New York Times. Large public libraries usually have microfiche for the Times.

You can find a wealth of information this way—both financial and social—about people who are influential on a national scale.

Directories

There are also numerous directories that give information about notable people, including:

- Who's Who in America
- Who's Who in Politics
- Webster's American Biographies
- Directory of National Biography
- Finance in Industry
- Contemporary Newsmakers

The Encyclopedia of Associations gives information about people according to their profession.

The Dun & Bradstreet Million Dollar Directory of America's Leading Public & Private Companies, provides information on more than 175,000 top businesses. There's also the *Macmillan Directory of Leading Private Companies.*

The *Standard & Poor Register of Corporations* provides detailed information on top businesses, including the names of the chairman of the board and all other officers; the company's bank, accountants, law firm, sales volume, and number of employees.

12 | *Getting the Relationship You Want*

It's up to you to determine how you are treated in a relationship. Sex, companionship, family matters, and money are only a few of the things you'll need to negotiate when you're getting into a relationship.

Your Expectations

Don't you wish that love relationships were as easy to deal with as friendships? No hassles, few fights, with everything running smoothly?

But friendships are easier to deal with because there's less at stake. You have lots of friends who fulfill various needs.

You can weight down a budding relationship when you make the mistake of expecting your mate to fulfill all of the complex things wrapped up in your image of the "ideal" relationship.

Instead of waiting for someone else to do the "right" things, then becoming discouraged when they don't—be appreciative of what you have. Then work toward everything you want.

Set Standards

Establish certain standards for your dates, and do it right

from the beginning. You're misleading yourself if you think that it will be easier to get someone to do what you want once they're hooked on you.

For this to work, you have to back up your own words. If someone isn't willing to pay your price for a relationship with you—whether that price is attention or expensive entertainments—then you must be prepared to look elsewhere.

For example, Matthew got involved with a woman who made it a habit to call right before she wanted to see him. It set a terrible precedent, and she naturally assumed that anytime she wanted to see him, she'd just have to call. Neither of them were happy with the arrangement—there was nothing for her to anticipate, while Matthew nurtured a secret resentment. Soon, their affair fizzled out.

If Matthew had set standards for his lover, she would never have started to use him as a "backup."

Ask for What You Want

If there are particular needs that aren't being met, then tell your lover specifically what you want. Do you want to spend more time together? Do you want to meet their friends? Do you want to be supported financially?

Ask for it. That's right, be blunt.

Successful people are used to negotiating for things. They know that they'll have to pay in one way or another for your company.

Ask for small things as well as big things—from a flower you can carry, to the key to their apartment. Ask for a phone call one night, and an impromptu champagne celebration the next.

You'll be respected for being honest and quite sure of yourself.

Women

Unfortunately, most women are taught to be manipulative in order to get what they want from men, rather than being forthright about their desires.

Women who are confident enough to outright ask for things are taken with the same seriousness that forthright men are.

How To Ask

The way you ask for things can be a powerful tool.

Instead of asking in a pleading way, state your request "I want to go sailing," or "Let's buy these shoes for when we go dancing."

Be lighthearted, without being childish. Don't make endless "hints" about what you want—that can become irritating. Ask outright, or put it out of your mind.

When you demand something or throw a tantrum, that puts you on a dependent and childish level. If you act sulky or cool when you don't get what you want, that puts your emotional equilibrium in the other person's hands.

Like anything else, asking for money is best done calmly and reasonably. Keep in mind that when you're asking for money, someone is buying rights to know about your financial condition. Be honest about your expenses, and your income.

Dealing with Refusal

You don't have the right to be angry with someone when they don't give you what you want. And don't take refusals as a cue to indulge in endless arguments about the nature of your relationship.

If someone is unwilling or incapable of doing what's necessary for the relationship to be healthy for you, then obviously you both need to move on. Nothing can overcome basic incompatibility.

Reguests That Benefit Them

Don't ask lightly—especially the first few times. Make sure you have a reason that includes *them* for wanting that dinner at the best restaurant or that new dress. Then, if you get turned down, you can say, "I was looking forward to a really special evening for us," or "It would be perfect for the party we're going to next week."

Then listen to their response. Sometimes people simply don't understand what you want. Find out what they *think* you're asking for, and what it means to them.

It's best when you can figure out a way that makes your request benefit them. If you're dating a woman who likes to look good in front of other people, point out what everyone will think of her taste. If you're dating a man who's after sex, expensive lingerie can be a good thing to ask for. Or if you want a vacation in the sun, talk about how good you'll both feel relaxing on the beach, walking in the moonlight by the ocean, sipping margaritas in the shade.

Gifts

People will consciously spend their money in ways to entice you. After all, it's natural for someone to use whatever they have in order to win your affection.

It's also true that people tend to value the things that cost the most. If someone is buying you expensive gifts or paying your rent, they are "investing" in you. This makes you more important to them, and it makes everything you do matter more.

To entice someone to give to you, you must be prepared to be on the "taking" end of the relationship.

Accepting Gifts

Be gracious when you accept the best service and gifts, but don't be surprised or overly excited when you get something you've asked for.

Instead, you should be confident that your potential mate will supply whatever you desire, since it is nothing more than you deserve.

Don't ever protest, "I couldn't take that!" when you're offered a large-ticket item like a trip or a car. If you act as if it's too much for them to offer, you may convince them. At the very least, you'll put the doubt in their mind.

Whenever someone gives you money, don't suggest that it's a loan. Quietly agree if they make a token suggestion, but don't mention when you're paying it back unless they ask.

Do show how much you love surprises. No matter what you get, a surprise gift should be appreciated double—for its inherent value, and the thought put into pleasing you without you having to ask.

You want to develop the habit of having your potential mate please you. So give something back when you're given a gift. A kiss or a hug is always positive reinforcement.

Refusing Gifts

When you don't want something, say no.

Don't let people buy you everything they want to, just for the sake of having things. Then there's no doubt that you'd take anything they offer. That tends to make people offer gifts less often.

Refuse gifts more in the beginning, but never give up the habit.

Be Discriminating

You don't have to act like a snob to make it clear you appreciate the best. That doesn't mean you demand better quality, but be discriminating in your appreciation of gifts.

Appreciate it when you are treated to the best. And if the choice is left to you, then choose the best. Not necessarily the most expensive things—but the best quality, and the most suitable for you. Even if you're dirt poor, your discriminating taste will be respected.

After dating several wealthy men, Jody learned that it worked to her advantage when she wasn't too easy to please.

She says that this kept her last lover on his toes, always ready to do more for her. For instance, early on he "casually" mentioned his empty apartment on the Upper East Side. Rather than rising to the bait, Jody offhandedly replied that she preferred to live on the Upper West Side.

Eventually, Jody's lover asked her to marry him, just to prove he'd give her the best he had to offer—himself.

Others' Expectations

If you feel pressured into doing things because you're accepting someone's gifts, then you're missing the entire point.

It takes two things to make a successful relationship—you have to feel free to give what you want, and you have to be satisfied with what you're getting.

Payment

Turn down gifts that clearly have strings attached. Be blunt about why you're refusing.

If you can be "bought," you're selling yourself for too little. Besides, once you start bargaining, then you're in competition with your potential mate. That means someone's going to lose.

Payback

Just because someone gives you money and gifts, that doesn't mean you're at their beck and call.

For example, if you give in and fetch the flowers for his

dinner party, soon he'll probably try to get you to pick up his dry cleaning. People naturally push things, just to see how far they can go.

Before you know it, you're reduced to the level of a servant instead of a potential mate.

Coercion

If gifts or money are thrown in your face as "prior payment" then immediately leave.

Then don't talk to that person for a while. You need to get some distance in order to rethink the entire relationship.

If the other person is serious about you, you'll know it from their subsequent pursuit and apologies. Even then, don't give in quickly. This is a vital point of respect and equality in your relationship, and is nonnegotiable.

"Selling" Yourself

Some people give money and gifts as an expression of their love, while others give things in lieu of love. They give because they think that absolves them of the need to give you their loyalty.

You'll know you're being bought, when:

1. The amount of money and value of gifts stays the same or diminishes. Your lover is probably viewing the relationship as a straight exchange— they're paying for your time and attention—and are trying to get a better "deal." You'll never get commitment from this person.
2. When you receive money or a gift when your lover breaks an engagement. It's the same thing as paying a lawyer or dentist when you've missed an appointment.
3. When you ask for more money or a larger-value gift than usual, and your lover responds with what you might do for them in gratitude.

4. When someone offers to "lend" you expensive clothes or jewelry to wear. It's insulting to let someone dress you up like you were a mannequin in a window. If it's not a gift, don't take a loan.

On the other hand, if gifts continue to grow in value the longer you are together, then that shows serious interest.

The same is true if someone lets you use their credit card. It creates a permanent record of your association, and other people see the bills—secretaries, accountants.

As one woman once said, "You know a man isn't hiding you from his wife when he lets you buy four pairs of shoes at Bloomingdale's with his Mastercard."

Being Supported

You walk a particularly fine line between independence and dependence when someone is financially supporting you.

At the very least, you may be letting yourself in for criticism and instructional advice as to how you live your life. You also may have to compromise on vital issues like the amount of time you spend together.

Don't ever allow someone to curtail your contact with other people until they've also given you a similar commitment.

And don't make a commitment unless you have what you want—whether it's marriage or the freedom of living apart and being supported.

You are the only person who can determine if you're giving up too much for too little. And you can only do that by being absolutely true to your purpose in life. Don't make the mistake of settling for someone who gives you the trappings of your goal, instead of the substance.

13 | *Common Relationship Pitfalls*

How important is a rich mate to you? The only way you can "sell out" is to chose a mate who doesn't meet your needs.

Don't depend on other people to make your life the way you want it. You have nothing to lose but a relationship that isn't satisfying you.

Deferring Your Happiness

If you find yourself thinking of how your relationship will be in the future, when your love grows, you're not paying attention to what's actually going on.

You must be satisfied with the way people treat you *now*. If you aren't, it's up to you to take action.

For example, one woman was involved in a quasirelationship with a man for almost a year—Sandra got together with him at least once a month to have sex. Sandra wasn't sure if she was interested in more with this man, but she wasn't really satisfied. It wasn't until she started being blunt with her lover—telling him she wanted to do other things together—that their relationship really began to develop.

Unfortunately, the relationship didn't lead to marriage, and Sandra says now that she regrets the amount of time she let go by. She hesitated to act for fear of losing the light-hearted sexual affair that was satisfying *some* of her needs. But the frustration had become too much to bear, and when she did have a chance to become more intimate, it was too late.

Incompatibility

First, make sure you're dealing with real problems— don't let your niggling worries and irritations get in the way of seeing what's truly bothering you.

Most people would rather focus on molehills rather than mountains, and you can spend years fighting and compromising on small things before you work your way to down basic issues of incompatibility.

Discuss your needs, while making it clear that you intend to find a relationship that gives you what you deserve. Be calm and reasonable. You can't demand love or respect from anyone, be it a date, a lover, or your mate.

Distance Yourself

If you're still bothered by fundamental things in the relationship after discussing the problem with your potential mate, then you have to distance yourself. Otherwise, it's easy to get stuck in a useless power struggle.

Move the relationship to a less intimate level by spending less time together. Give both yourselves time to cool off and get the situation in perspective.

Bill realized he was deluding himself after he pursued a woman for almost a year. The relationship developed rapidly in the beginning, then he found himself in a role of escort/ lover, always on call for her social events. Though he struggled to become more intimate with her, even asking her to marry him at one point, she held him off. It wasn't until he started pulling away that she made some effort to give him what he needed.

As it turned out, Bill's lover wasn't willing to become

partners with him. Without knowing it, he had a completely different attitude about the relationship that she did.

So if you don't feel it's moving forward, then you're the one who needs time and distance to rethink things.

Settling

If you keep trying to make someone else change to suit you, you may win battles but you'll never win the war.

People typically stay in a relationship that isn't working for far too long, trying to make it fit their needs or betting on the future potential. But this isn't a gambling spree.

You're building a foundation for the rest of your life. Do you really want to settle for something that isn't satisfying you?

When you stay in a situation simply because it's better than any alternative you can think of, you're cheating yourself of the opportunities you'd have if you were free.

Get out and give yourself a chance to find someone who really suits you.

Pleasing Potential Mates

It's natural to do things for someone you love. By making them feel better with you than with anyone else, you become the most important person in their lives.

Do things you know they'll appreciate—talk about their interests, plan surprises for them, and learn to compromise.

But don't make the mistake of catering to their every desire or trying to anticipate what they want. After all, your potential mate was attracted to you for the way you are, not for the person that you try to become for them.

Changing Your Behavior

Don't change your behavior in order to get someone to love you.

Taking up tennis so you can play together every weekend or jogging with your potential mate every morning may seem like a way to strengthen your bond—even if you aren't very interested in those activities.

But that's the very thing that will cause the destruction of the relationship.

For a while, it may feel like there's harmony—but you're really living another person's life. You're creating an illusion of a relationship rather than building a foundation between two real people.

Deferring to Their Choices

Don't fall into the habit of deferring to other people's choices. Compromise means that both of you give in occasionally.

Frank learned this when he fell in love with a beautiful heiress, and was willing to do anything to please her. He even changed his shower schedule while they were on a trip, because she thought it made more sense to shower in the morning rather than at night. Now Frank says, "I wish I'd told her I preferred to shower at night. No matter what hassles were involved with sex and sleeping...."

He realized later how much he'd allowed her to hound him into doing personal things her way. In doing so, Frank built an illusion of a relationship that wasn't able to survive the test of time.

In the end you'll always be more disappointed and frustrated than if you'd stayed true to your own preferences.

Arguing

You have to work together to solve the problems in a relationship, and that means you have to cooperate for communication to take place.

When a problem comes up, the first thing to do is remember that you're both on the same side—after all, you've gotten this far together.

How to Argue

When something goes wrong, talk about it. Don't simmer or indulge in blame or simply vent your feelings. Contrary to our instinctive "fight back" response, this doesn't balance the scale or solve the problem.

And don't expect your potential mate to fix everything you don't like. Since you can't demand anything, you can't rest your peace of mind on your mate's compliance.

Only complain if you're willing to do something yourself to make things better. That way you're working together on a problem instead of forcing it into someone else's lap.

Cooperate and Compromise

You must remember that you can't pass judgment on anyone else's choices—you can only observe and see patterns. Whatever their reasons are for doing things, they've chosen to do what's best for them.

Besides, if you're too busy insisting that you're right, you won't be able to find ways to compromise.

Merryl realized this when she became engaged to a successful entrepreneur. When her fiance said he wanted to postpone the wedding to the fall rather than June, the resulting argument almost broke them apart permanently. Merryl says she had a hundred reasons for getting married in June, and was secretly worried he was having second thoughts.

Luckily, she went home and cooled off before irreparable damage was done. When they talked later, Merryl put aside her paranoia and listened to her fiance's reasons. Though he'd already said the postponement was due to business scheduling, she found out then that he wanted to delay so he could take a couple of months off for their honeymoon.

Merryl says she almost missed out on something special because she was too busy insisting on having things exactly her way. After all, they were getting married, and having the wedding she'd always dreamed of—and to her those were the most important things.

By respecting other people's choices, you allow communication to open up between you. Then you can cooperate and compromise.

Ultimatums

Don't put the relationship on the line when you argue. The time to make it clear you intend to get what you want is before or after an argument, not during.

Nobody likes threats, and presenting an ultimatum in the heat of the moment usually backfires. Even if the other person wants to give in, it's likely they'll stick to their position out of pride, if nothing else.

Plus, every time you use that threat—"I'll leave!"—it carries less weight. Eventually, it means nothing at all. You don't want the status of your relationship to be unimportant.

When They're Angry

If your potential mate is the one to express uncertainty about the relationship, don't use that as your cue to freak out.

Be calm and confident that you both will resolve things. Reinforce the positive aspects of your relationship as you discuss the problems.

One of the best ways to control your defensive reactions is by focusing on your own priorities. Someone else's displeasure is easier to put in perspective if you're confident about your own desires.

It can also help you focus on the real issues trying to attain your driving purpose in life instead of being sidetracked into mundanity.

When to Stop Arguing

Don't ever allow yourself to be drawn into arguments that

make you feel belittled or abused. If you repeatedly feel put down, then stop arguing. Either ask for the behavior to end, or leave.

Bitter arguing simply tells people you're willing to stick around even though you're unhappy. Nobody respects that.

Prior Relationships

Meet as many of your potential mate's family members, friends, and associates as you can. The more involved you become in someone's life, the more important you become.

Pay attention to the interpersonal relationships among the family. Mothers are particularly important for both men and women—notice the things your potential mate admires about them, as well as what they dislike.

Don't ever try to alienate your lover from the people he or she is close to. Discover qualities in friends and family that you can appreciate. Don't go overboard, but be pleasant and helpful until you can find things you truly have in common.

Ex-Spouses and Lovers

Listen to what people say about their past primary relationships. The things they complain about in particular—not as indicators of what you should avoid, but for the insecurities they reveal. Did she withhold sex? Did he put her down?

These are things your potential mate hated, but it was also the problem they kept trying to fix. In a way, the problem became the relationship. And it was something that was obviously never resolved.

Accept that fact, and even when your potential mate gets aggravated or emotional over an ex-spouse or lover, you don't have to let it bother you. It's simply old habits that will probably never die as long as they have contact with each other.

It will only have bearing on you and your relationship if you allow it to. Arguing about current interactions is the only thing that will make it important *now*.

Your Past Relationships

Whatever you do, don't compare your potential mate to people from past relationships, even if it's positive. No one appreciates being judged.

When you do talk about your ex-lovers, don't constantly complain about them. If you try to pin all the blame on them, no matter what terrible things they did, it only sounds like sour grapes. There were two of you in the relationship, and inevitably, part of the problem was yours.

You can also look like a fool for putting up with their behavior. You don't need to tell a potential mate how badly you handled everything the last time around.

So do yourself a favor and remember the good points about your previous relationships. Emphasize the things you learned, and the fun you had. If you can't think of anything good, then you need to rethink your whole approach to relationships.

Jealousy

When you feel threatened or jealous, then you're often comparing yourself to someone that your potential mate has singled out for attention. You're questioning your own worth and the worth of your relationship, over actions they probably think are unimportant.

You're allowing someone else to control your reactions, when you try to reconfirm your potential mate's desire and/ or faithfulness.

Why give other people that much power over you? It trivializes the commitments you've made to each other. And it implies a basic lack of trust.

Admire People

Instead, admire attractive people of your own sex along with your lover.

This can be particularly effective for women.

When you see a pretty woman look at your mate or flirt with him, point it out. Does it sound crazy? Well, you'll never stop a man from looking at other women by disliking it.

Enjoying desirability with him, instead of making it something he has to hide or feel guilty about, is the way to win his heart.

After all, our society has trained men to be more visually responsive while women respond better to verbal signals. It's just one of the ways boys and girls become conditioned as they grow up.

By openly acknowledging that your lover enjoys looking at pretty women, and by accepting his reaction, you are subtly bringing his response into the area that you are better trained in—talking about it. In effect, you are guiding his natural impulses toward communication, something that will make you feel more comfortable.

In turn, your lover will feel like he has his cake and can eat it, too. You have allowed him to look and watch. You can even bring an attractive woman to his attention. What man wouldn't treasure that?

In fact, if you can master this simple form of giving, you'll find your lover is much more open to you, both sexually as well as emotionally.

Employees

The way you interact with employees and domestic staff can help determine your own status.

Assuming Authority

Whatever you do, don't make the mistake of assuming

that you're the boss, too, since you're dating the boss.

Until you're married, anyone who works closely with your potential mate has more influence than you do. They have more access, and they know him better. It doesn't take much to imply disdain, and employees will have plenty of opportunities to express theirs—about you—if they wish.

For example, don't be overbearing or officious about asking your lover's secretary to do things for you—from buying theater tickets to putting your calls through to him. All it would take is a few well-timed comments along the lines of "Quite the little wife..." for your potential mate to be wary of your attentions.

Be Discreet

It's always best to treat employees with the respect that professionals deserve.

Be friendly, but don't assume friendship too quickly. Employees will be compelled to treat you nicely since you're dating the boss, but their personal feelings aren't always in step with their smiles.

If an employee makes overtures of friendship, don't be fooled. They could be interested in finding out "the real scoop" on you, and wouldn't mind letting your potential mate know what they think.

Also—never ask employees questions about your potential mate. It shows weakness, and usually gives you no information of any importance. If information is offered, take it with a huge grain of salt, and don't encourage more disclosures.

Instead, keep your conversations pleasant and impersonal. Don't ever confide your feelings for your potential mate, or details of what happens between you. Not the gifts or trips or dinners—employees should only know what their boss tells them.

14 | *Love and Sex*

Even if you and your potential mate are compatible, you may not have exactly the same ideas of what goes into "love."

Desire

What is desire? When you long for someone's presence and their touch, that's desire—and it can run rampant over every part of your life if you let it.

Usually, the feelings associated with passionate desire are rife with uncertainties—Does she love me? Am I making him happy? Am I good or attractive or smart enough?

Most people equate desire with love. And they want to be desired in return.

It's that pit-of-the-stomach feeling that leaves you deliriously on edge. Just make sure you don't fall off that edge.

Stand firm. Love is something that takes time and trust. It can only grow as you get to know each other.

Romance

What is romance? For many people, it's the affection and attention, driven by sexual desire, that has come to symbolize love.

Romance directly supports the emotional side of a relationship. It's not the stuff to base a lifetime on, but it sure makes things spicy.

Be Romantic

The best way to get romance in your life is by freely giving it. Do the sort of things things you would like to receive in return. You don't have to be flamboyant or contrived, but allow your quirky side to run free.

Do even the silly, romantic things. Gifts, notes, and flowers can be an affirmation of your bond. Encourage taking trips together—not necessarily business trips, but short vacation weekends. You can cement your relationship through playful activity, and become associated in your lover's mind with pleasure.

Most of all, provide opportunities for romance to flourish by staying open to new things. Make sure you shake up the routine every once in a while.

Affection

Affection is nonsexual intimacy. Used wisely, affection ate contact can do more toward developing a relationship than anything else.

Respond to your lover's touch, but don't always allow it to turn into sex. There must be hugs and caresses outside of sex or you'll both be deprived of the emotional bond that enriches a relationship.

Be Affectionate

You won't get affection by asking for it. You have to give it to get it.

If you only touch your lover when you want sex, your relationship won't be very affectionate. If you aren't interested in stroking his hair or cuddling together on the couch, he probably won't be interested in touching you either. And if you don't want to take the effort to cover her feet with a blanket, or to fetch a glass of milk, she won't do the same for you.

It's also good to be quietly attentive to your lover in front of other people, as well as in private. Gently affirming your bond in public can have a positive affect on the way your relationship is treated by others.

Sex

Passionate sex is not love. It's passionate sex, with all the wonderful feelings that stimulates inside us.

Delay

It's best not to have sex as soon as a potential lover gets interested in you. Once someone starts wanting to be more intimate, a little frustration can go a long, long way. They'll get used to trying to please you, while they're trying to win you.

There's a wonderful scene in *The Player* where the producer takes the "ice queen" he's been pursuing to a fancy celebrity fund-raiser, and afterwards, he kisses her and asks if she's ready to have sex with him yet. She responds with a warm and passionate kiss, and smiling, says, "Soon..." It's as if she can't wait, but she can't bring herself to be intimate with someone *that* quickly.

What does he do? He responds with an offer to go to Alcapulco for the weekend. By waiting, she got more and more from him, and her worth only grew in his estimation. By the end of the story, he winds up marrying her.

Set Standards

If you decide to have sex before you've set certain standards or agreed to specific commitments, you have to realize you're agreeing to casual sex.

Of course, the next time you may decide differently. You may not want to maintain a sexual relationship unless certain commitments are made and questions of monogamy are settled. But you'll have to be the one to make that clear. Your lover is going to be assuming casual sex is fine with you.

Whatever you do, don't trade sex for gifts. That sets up a service relationship, with you on the servicing end. Remember, the rich got rich by being good with money. Pretty soon, you'll end up bargaining over how much money they give for how much service you give. That's a no-win situation for you.

Talking About Sex

Most people shy away from talking about sex. That's because we're taught to keep our most intimate and personal responses private. Since we aren't used to discussing these things with people, it's sometimes difficult to remember that we're *supposed* to talk about our sexuality with our lover.

Both of you need to keep open minds. You must open up yourself, and be prepared to hear things you might not expect in order to draw out a person's true feelings about sex.

Discovering Their Turn-ons

There's no way of knowing if we're fulfilling our lover's needs unless we talk about what turns them on.

That doesn't mean asking, "Did you enjoy that?" after a sexual encounter. That's begging for affirmation instead of seeking an honest response.

You can use a number of indirect methods to open up the discussion—such as books, movies, games, etc. But don't tease someone about sexual things they do or don't do. Teasing isn't talking, it's a subtle form of condescension and that's the quickest way to inhibit someone.

Revealing Your Turn-ons

Use any opportunity you can to tell your lover what turns you on, whether it's a fantasy or a real encounter.

Hints and innuendo just don't work when it comes to sex. Talk about the things you've done together that you like, and point out variations that might be even more fun.

Things to Avoid

Don't fall into the trap of only talking about sex when you have a problem. If it's always negative then eventually neither one of you will want to talk about sex much less have it.

And try not to get sidetracked into other areas of your relationship while you're talking about sex.

Karen realized she'd been doing this only after she left her lover. She says she equated their hurried morning sex with a feeling of being used. Whenever she tried to talk about other ways they could have sex, she ended up dragging in other incidents in their relationship to prove her point. After a while, she couldn't bear to have sex with her lover at any time.

Karen put too much weight on something that was a simple preference or habit for her lover, and that made them unable to deal calmly with it.

Inhibitions

You and your lover needn't engage in any acts you don't want to, but you owe it to each other to explore the way each of you feels.

You also owe it to each other to not judge sexual preferences as immoral or perverted. Just as you could never completely understand sexual intercourse when you were a virgin, you won't be able to understand any variation you haven't tried or fantasized about.

Your Inhibitions

Ideally, sex should be a welcome and fulfilling part of your life. When you consider sex a natural thing, you are better able to communicate about it, and you will probably enjoy a broader range of experience in your sexual encounters.

But if you have inhibitions about certain sex acts, or are uncomfortable with sexuality, then in order to have a fulfilling sexual experience you must discuss these delicate issues with your lover. Allowing someone to see your intimate secrets can do more toward freeing your sexuality than anything else.

If you can keep an open mind, and are able to trust your partner, there's a good chance you'll be surprised by your own reactions.

Your Lover's Inhibitions

If your lover is hesitant about doing something sexual, they may simply be unsure of themselves. Maybe they've never done it before, and don't want to be awkward or bad at it. Or maybe they don't want to admit it's something new.

Be understanding and tolerant of your lover's fears. By gently helping them break through the barriers that stop them from a fulfilling sex life, you will be essential to their happiness.

Experiment

Your primary responsibility during a sexual encounter is to be open and honest. It is a mutual experience, and it will be complete only if both of you work together.

Even little things can keep your sexual encounters exciting, like having sex at different times and in different places. And don't always do the same routine.

Exchanging Power

Play around with the different ways of giving and receiving pleasure—paying attention to your lover's entire body.

Have entire encounters with one partner completely giving and touching and stimulating, while the other lies back and relaxes. Next time, switch it around.

You don't need to keep a mental tally sheet of who's done what to whom, trading fellatio for cunnilingus, for example. And don't feel like you have to even up the score every time your lover gives you a massage. Sex is a mutual act, and the power exchange should flow in a continuous, harmonious cycle.

Fantasies

From daydreams to images that go through your mind as you masturbate, you can use your fantasies to help stimulate your sexual response.

Fantasies often deal with taboos or things that we would never consider doing in real life. But that's what fantasies are—an outlet for sexual impulses that are not acceptable to society. You certainly don't have to govern or censor your own fantasies. It's a product of the twisting and shaping you go through during the development of your personality.

Understanding and accepting yourself is the key to sexual fulfillment. By being completely honest and willing to explore your most basic reactions you'll find you also uncover the things that motivate you in the rest of your life, as well.

Ask About Their Fantasies

Often a person's fantasies are the truest indicator of their desires. If you encourage your lover to reveal their innermost fantasies, you'll know exactly what to do to turn them on. Most people will start out with a very simple, "acceptable" fantasy since fear of rejection is very real where sex is concerned.

Your main task is to be nonjudgmental and encouraging. It's also best to stay objective rather than directly relating the discussion to the sex you're having.

Reveal Your Fantasies

The easiest way to get your lover to discuss their fantasies is by confessing some of yours. With such an intimate topic, people instinctively feel better if there is a balance struck in the information that is revealed.

Since we are taught to hide our sexuality, you may not be completely aware of your own fantasies. They can unwind in your mind on nearly a subliminal level, with certain undefined images of bodies, actions, and attitudes that trigger your sexual response.

Look for patterns or certain images that seem similar. What sort of sex acts turn you on? Or do you enjoy thinking about scenes of domination, humiliation, submission, and even taboos....

Even if you're not sure what exactly is turning you on, try to explain it to your lover. Not only will your discussion deepen your intimacy and improve sex, but you'll gain a much greater understanding of yourself at the same time.

The trust involved in sharing fantasies will help form a basis for a real and loving relationship.

Primary Fantasy

Often people develop a certain fantasy that they return to over and over again. Habits like the "Saturday Evening Missionary Position" type of sex can be considered a sexual ritual. In much the same way, other people get their satisfaction from sexual fetishes, such as responding to high heels.

When you indulge in behavior to the exclusion of other

forms of sexual expression, you're taking the easy way out.

But by sharing your primary fantasy with someone, you open yourself up to all kinds of variations on that theme— as well as discovering new things to enjoy.

Role Playing

Once you've starting talking about your fantasies, the natural thing is to incorporate some of the elements into your sexual encounters.

Many people find that they experience a sense of release by acting out their fantasies. It's also a good way to introduce a wider range of experiences into your sexual encounters.

For example, Jack found out that his lover was turned on by the idea of being a harem girl, but she resisted discussing this fantasy because she felt it was "wrong" to imagine herself being a slave. But one evening, when she complained of being scratched by his stubbly beard, he suggested that she shave him. He says that she was hesitant at first— because she'd never shaved a man before—but she ended up adoring it. Especially near the end when he called her his "little harem girl."

She was able to indulge in her nurturing/servicing desires without feeling as if she was giving up her equality.

Be Inventive

If you always wanted to tie up your lover, a nonthreatening way to suggest it is by describing a bondage fantasy that appeals to you. Then suggest you do it.

Role playing can also be as easy as deciding that one of you is to be the sexual aggressor, and that the other will be seduced. Or you can pick different personalities, character types from movies or stereotypes, and see what happens when you come together. Use clothes or props or anything else that comes to hand.

Go Slowly

Do keep in mind that not all fantasies are meant to be acted out.

If you or your lover are uncomfortable with the idea, then it's best to keep the topic on a discussion level rather than trying to hurry the process. You'll always have time to explain in greater detail what excites you if you don't push it.

But if you are nonjudgemental and understanding of each other, then acting out your fantasies will be an exciting, intriguing experience. You'll find it's a gateway to a more fulfilling sexuality.

15 | *Commitments*

When you make a monogamous commitment to someone, you are relying on them to provide you with what you need—whether it's a certain level of income, attention, or sexual satisfaction.

You may think that by marrying or agreeing to be monogamous you'll get the things you want. But the commitment itself means nothing unless your specific needs are being met right *now*.

Keep Dating

Don't ever make a commitment to be monogamous until your lover meets your criteria for a monogamous relationship. If it's marriage you want, then date other people until you are engaged. If it's full financial support, then that's what you must get before you stop dating.

Be honest, but don't flaunt your other dates in your lover's face. Just the fact that you are "available" until you find someone who gives you what you deserve, will enable you to get it.

Even if you both are crazy about each other—you can't close the option of seeing other people until you get the commitment you want. Otherwise, you're giving up control over whether your needs will be satisfied.

Settling

You'll never get what you want by giving yourself away lightly.

Even if your goal is to be in a monogamous relationship, don't try to force every person you date into the mold of your potential mate. You run the risk giving up what you really want for a certain level of commitment.

A good thing to keep in mind when you're dating a wealthy person is the first question of the marriage vows— "...for richer or poorer?"

Everybody has the potential to go bust. If you couldn't see yourself marrying this person if they didn't have money, then don't get married.

Be Independent

In order to get the relationship you deserve, you must be prepared to live alone rather than settle for less. As long as you keep pursuing your true goal, you have a chance to achieve it.

That's the secret to getting the relationship you want— not elaborate games of "bait and switch."

Instead of being afraid of being lonely and forcing a relationship along, take the time alone to work out your personal anxieties. In the end, it's better to grimly hang on and struggle to fulfill your own life, than waste time rushing around trying to find someone who can.

Discussing the Commitment You Want

When you're dating, be honest about the sort of relationship you want. Otherwise, you'll be sending mixed signals, and will appear indecisive.

Talk about relationships that you admire, and be clear about the sort of things you would appreciate. But don't go overboard. If you want children, that doesn't mean you constantly point out cute little tykes and sigh over Gerber commercials.

Arguing About Commitments

Don't ever try to convince someone to give you the commitment you want. Begging for love or arguing about behavior will not make you more desirable.

Instead, be resolute about the sort of commitment you want. And know that, whether it's from this person or not, you'll get it. The only question is how much you'll put up with until you decide to end something that isn't satisfying you.

It may sound cold, but you might as well be practical about it—at this point, if you aren't getting what you want, you have to get out.

Things to Avoid

There are certain signs when you're involved in a relationship that is counterproductive.

Abuse

Never make a commitment to someone who doesn't respect you. If your potential mate is dishonest with you, or they hurt you physically or emotionally, then get out of the relationship.

If you feel intimidated or belittled, it will only get worse with time. Many people make the mistake of thinking that marriage will make everything better. But why should it? There's no reason for your mate to try any harder—in fact, it's just the opposite. You're both more likely to be fighting to get whatever you can.

If you agreed to marry under negative circumstances, the human temptation will be for your mate to push things to see just how far they can go.

Competition

When you compare yourself to your mate, you start to compete with each other.

Competition can lead to resentments, subtle put-downs, and obsessive regard of small matters. Don't be tempted to tally up personal wins and losses. Once you start competing, you're inevitably rooting for the defeat of your mate.

Isolation

If someone you're dating doesn't like to be seen in public places with you, then they aren't likely to commit themselves to you.

The same goes for when you travel—you may go places together, but does your potential mate introduce you to their friends? Or do they take you to "out-of-the-way" places?

If you are isolated from your lover's circles of friends, then you aren't really part of their life.

Living Together

If you want to get married, set a date before you move in together. It can even be as vague as "a year from spring."

Don't assume that once you're living together, marriage will come next.

You'll find yourself in a losing position if you're living with someone who says they love you, but just can't commit to marriage. That leaves you depending on them to come around, while they have no reason to even try. They've got you exactly where they want you—why should they give you any more?

16 | *Getting Married*

As far as weddings go, remember that elaborate celebrations are for first-time brides. Yet it's considered acceptable for men to participate in a formal wedding even if they have been married before.

Once your engagement is announced, preparations for the wedding can begin. Since this involves volumes of things to consider, consult a bridal consultant, or bridal magazine, or any of the numerous social guides to proper weddings.

Eloping

If you absolutely must have a huge wedding, then by all means, go for it. But don't ignore the benefits of a lovely, spontaneous wedding.

Men are typically more impatient with the necessary arrangements involved in a wedding. If your lover is reluctant or hesitates, a flight to Mexico with the promise of sun and fun can be more of an enticement than trying to get him to plan a formal occasion.

In the same way you won't "prove" your love by doing things, don't ask your lover to prove it to you. Sticking on something like a big wedding could damage the relationship before it's really gotten started.

Later on, after you're married, you can throw huge formal parties and shine to your heart's content.

Engagements

The engagement ring is traditionally worn for the first time at the announcement of your engagement.

But an engagement ring is not necessary—if anyone asks, you can say you've postponed making the choice until you decide what kind of wedding band you want. Or, you can say you're getting a jeweled wedding band. Or say you don't intend to wear one.

Engagement Party

The best day for the engagement party is the day before the engagement is announced in the newspaper. Since most papers announce engagements in their Sunday edition, have the party on Saturday.

A simple cocktail party is enough. Make sure you have champagne on hand so at one point in the evening, all the guests can make a toast to the couple.

You can also have favors that incorporate your joint initials (book matches, napkins).

If it's your second wedding, it's better to call the announcement party simply a "party" rather than an engagement party.

Invitations

You can handwrite the invitations on good quality notepaper (either white or cream-colored). If you want the announcement to be a surprise, don't mention anything about the engagement in the invitation.

If you want people to know it's an engagement party, you can write "in honor of Stacey Smith and Brad Jones" beneath the line that reads you are inviting people "to cocktails" or "to a reception."

Engagement Announcement

Contact your local newspaper to find out their policy

about announcing engagements. Usually they want it at least ten days in advance.

Follow the format printed in the paper: the names of the affianced pair; your home towns; date of the wedding (either specific or general; e.g., next spring"); the names of both of your schools; your parents' professions; both of your occupations, and special honors in your career.

In bigger cities like New York, Los Angeles, and Chicago, the main newspaper doesn't announce very many engagements. Make sure to send your announcement to a local alternative as well.

Unless it's your first wedding, the newspaper will usually print engagement announcement only if one or both of you are prominent in the city.

Prenuptial Agreements

Prenuptial agreements plan for the end of a marriage, so it's not the most pleasant thing to be thinking about while you're planning the happy occasion.

But don't be taken aback if you are presented with a prenuptial agreement before you go through with the wedding ceremony. People with wealth are used to dealing with contracts, so it is natural that their lawyers will suggest drawing up a prenuptial agreement.

Consult a Lawyer

If you are presented with a prenuptial agreement, you owe it to yourself to have a lawyer look at it. After all, your fiance arranged with his or her lawyer to draw up the agreement. If only in the interest of equality, you must do the same.

Immediately signing an agreement shows how little you value yourself. The only way to maintain your dignity is to treat the agreement as seriously as a business contract. After all, your potential mate is agreeing to give you a substantial amount of money if the marriage doesn't work out.

Breaking a Prenuptial Agreement

No matter what a prenuptial agreement says, it isn't ironclad. Agreements can be overruled on charges of:

1. Duress—if you were coerced into signing at the last minute.
2. Unfairness—when one person gets disproportionately more than the other.
3. Misrepresentation—when one mate didn't fully reveal their assets and financial position.
4. Fraud—when one mate deliberately defrauds the other.

Making Your Decision

Have your lawyer explain the agreement to you. You'll want to know how well your potential mate is willing to treat you even if things don't work out. A small settlement says they have little faith in you, and it might even indicate their treatment of you during the marriage.

If you can't agree with the terms of the prenuptial agreement—don't sign it. Not because of what may happen if you split up, but because you're accepting your potential mate's attitude about the relationship.

Point out exactly what you don't like, and negotiate to make the agreement more satisfying to you.

If the agreement is held over you as an either/or situation, then walk away. Never let anyone coerce you into marriage.

In the end, you have to consider every point about your potential mate when it comes time to get married. Trust your instincts, stay focused on your purpose in life, and get out there and find the mate you deserve.

Index